More praise for *Big Boards for Families* by Sandy Coughlin . . .

"Sandy's love for food and entertaining is contagious and this book is full of fun and creative ideas. I can't wait to recreate these special spreads for future holidays, parties, and special occasions."
— Maria Lichty, author of *Two Peas & Their Pod Cookbook*

"In *Big Boards for Families* Sandy Coughlin masters how to create stunning charcuterie boards that are approachable and absolutely delicious. I guarantee everyone will run to the table for these."
— Jocelyn Delk Adams, award-winning cookbook author of *Grandbaby Cakes*

"Sandy has mastered the art of effortless entertaining by seamlessly marrying creative, wholesome foods with the joy of dining and gathering together. Her boards are inspiring, easy to customize, and the perfect way to mix up mealtime for kids and adults alike."
— Kelly Senyei, author of *The Secret Ingredient Cookbook* and founder of Just a Taste

"Simplifies every meal while making you look like a cooking genius! You'll refer back to this book forever."
— Myquillyn Smith, *New York Times* best-selling author of *Welcome Home*

"Sandy's creative boards are not only gorgeous, they inspire you to gather precious hearts and souls around the table to celebrate life together in a simple yet memorable way!"
—Melissa Michaels, *New York Times* best-selling author of *Simple Gathering*s, *Dwelling* and *The Inspired Room*

"Sandy's magical gift is bringing people and especially families together surrounded by big boards of gorgeous food."
—Catherine McCord, author and founder of *One Potato*

"If you've ever wondered how to put together a big, beautiful, welcoming spread of food for family or friends, read this book!"
— Elise Bauer, founder of Simply Recipes

"The creativity contained within *Big Boards for Families* is truly inspirational! This is an instant classic that will bring people to the table to create memorable meals."
— Lori Lange, founder of RecipeGirl.com

BIG
BOARDS
FOR
FAMILIES

Healthy, Wholesome Charcuterie Boards and Food Spread
Recipes That Bring Everyone Around the Table

SANDY COUGHLIN
CREATOR OF *RELUCTANT ENTERTAINER*

FAIR WINDS

Inspiring | Educating | Creating | Entertaining

Brimming with creative inspiration, how-to projects, and useful information to enrich your everyday life, Quarto Knows is a favorite destination for those pursuing their interests and passions. Visit our site and dig deeper with our books into your area of interest: Quarto Creates, Quarto Cooks, Quarto Homes, Quarto Lives, Quarto Drives, Quarto Explores, Quarto Gifts, or Quarto Kids.

First Published in 2021 by Fair Winds Press, an imprint of The Quarto Group,
100 Cummings Center, Suite 265-D, Beverly, MA 01915, USA.
T (978) 282-9590 F (978) 283-2742 QuartoKnows.com

Fair Winds Press titles are also available at discount for retail, wholesale, promotional, and bulk purchase. For details, contact the Special Sales Manager by email at specialsales@quarto.com or by mail at The Quarto Group, Attn: Special Sales Manager, 100 Cummings Center, Suite 265-D, Beverly, MA 01915, USA.

25 24 23 22 21   2 3 4 5

ISBN: 978-0-76037-166-4

Digital edition published in 2021
eISBN: 978-0-76037-167-1

Library of Congress Control Number: 2021939679

Design and page Layout: Laura Klynstra
Photography: Abigail Coughllin

Printed in China

To *The Big Board* and *Reluctant Entertainer* communities, this book is for you! Without your loyalty and support, this book would never have been possible.

To my talented daughter and photographer, Abby, with your beautiful touch, every day you inspire me!

CONTENTS

CHAPTER 1

Bring Your Family Around the Table

"Become friends with people who aren't your age. Hang out with people whose first language isn't the same as yours. Get to know someone who doesn't come from your social class. This is how you see the world. This is how you grow."

—ROUMAISSA

Probably every parent of grown children can look back and think about things they wish they'd done differently. But this quote reminds me of something we definitely did *right* over the years—create meaningful table experiences for and with our kids. At the family table, we exposed our children to a variety of flavors, people, ideas, and viewpoints. We also taught them about hospitality—the gift of making others feel warm and welcome. That's certainly not the only aspect to good parenting, but it's a great place to start!

Now, years later, making boards is one of the best and easiest ways I know to foster connection, model hospitality, and create meaningful table experiences for your family. All you need is a board, a few tools, and some favorite family recipes to get started. A board with a lip ensures the food won't fall off, so it won't be a frustrating experience—in fact, it'll be quite fun! With just a little effort and inspiration, which is what I hope to provide in these pages, you'll be able to create meals that bring your family together to share experiences, ideas, and memories that last a lifetime.

IT ALL STARTS WITH FAMILY

From one generation to the next, in every country and culture, people come together around food boards. Why? Because the best memories always involve loved ones and delicious food.

At the family table, values are shaped, bodies are nourished, love is demonstrated, and, yes, it's where our senses etch all of those cherished moments in our minds forever. If you look back, that was likely true for you. It's certainly been true for me.

My mother loved to entertain and showed her love by feeding people—her family especially. For Mom, even simple meals were small celebrations, always made with love. It was a love she passed on to me and my family.

I started cooking at a young age. Later, as a wife and mom to three little ones, my skills expanded. So did my ability to stretch meals. Leftovers were golden, and I got savvy about using up everything in the fridge. I also realized the value of family meals. Our family was busy, just like yours. Mealtime gave us a chance to connect. Gathering at the table brings families together and keeps them close.

The same principles apply to friends, the ones who are so dear that they feel like family. Like my mom, feeding both family and friends is one of the ways I show love. I would never have imagined her legacy would lead me to start my blog, *Reluctant Entertainer,* dedicated to making hospitality a household word and encouraging people to feast on life. And I certainly never imagined how incorporating boards into my culinary repertoire would help so many people discover a fun, easy, appealing way to entertain friends, and feed families.

THE BEGINNINGS OF THE BIG BOARD

Four years ago, twelve of my friends visited my small, mountain home for a girlfriends' weekend. I wanted our first meal together to be extra special, so I decided to celebrate with a *big* charcuterie. We squeezed together on the back deck overlooking the trees to drink wine and feast on the biggest, most beautiful charcuterie you've ever laid eyes on! We nibbled on tortellini skewers, savory slices of salami, a rich, creamy assortment of cheese, and fresh bruschetta. Such a gorgeous spread!

My friends took a picture of me holding that beautiful board and shared it online. Before I knew it, "The Big Board" became a phenomenon. Since then, The Big Board has been used over and over, for every kind of meal and occasion to celebrate food and people. I've shared recipe after recipe on my blog, inspiring others to join in the experience.

In retrospect, I'm starting to understand why The Big Board became so popular. Boards are easy and fun for everyone. One of my core philosophies is this: you don't have to be a great cook or perfect hostess to entertain. That's what got me started on serving boards for dinners and special occasions.

Whether you're a trained chef or you've never cooked a day in your life, the 52 fabulous recipes I'm sharing with you here will help you create boards that your family will love. That's why I'm so excited about this book! *Big Boards for Families* is a book that says, "You can do this!"

MAKE A BOARD SPECIAL BY MAKING IT YOURS

The beauty of this book is the ease and versatility of making a board your own. You're feeding your family of five? Great! Make the whole recipe and have leftovers for tomorrow's lunch. Hosting ten for a holiday? Just double the recipe. A weeknight supper for three? Cut it in half. No matter how many, or how few, you're feeding, boards are fun to make and create a special vibe the minute you set them out.

Inside these pages, you will find fresh and flavorful, simple yet impressive boards to inspire meals and encourage connection. Each board recipe gives suggestions for cooking, assembling, shortcuts, and tips. And, as I always say, there's really no right or wrong. The spreads and boards in this book are meant to be used as a guide. Feel free to substitute and change up the ingredient list to suit your taste.

One tip for success: Read through the entire recipe and make a shopping list. Organization and preparation are key to making good boards. It also takes pressure off the cook!

BIG BOARDS ARE WHAT FAMILIES NEED NOW

I've so enjoyed creating Big Boards in our home, often working with my daughter, Abby, as she comes up with some of the most creative and wholesome boards. The Big Board can be a family project from beginning to delicious end!

Boards add a new element to mealtime, where so many of us are working from home now. At the end of a homeschool day, or when the kids get home from school, how special to change up a mundane meal and create a board together as a family? Board building and cooking together can also be used as a teaching tool for kids (counting, weighing, following directions, etc.).

Every board we make and meal we share gives us a chance to tell to our stories, making connections that run deep and new traditions and memories that last.

Ready to make your first food board for your family?

SIMPLE KITCHEN TOOLS

What I love about Big Boards is how versatile they are. You can customize them to meet the unique personality of your family, or you can serve a board for a special dinner for friends or neighbors, or even a fun appetizer night. The more you use them, the more you'll see how Big Boards fit so many occasions. I recommend starting with loved ones in your home, and with your favorite family recipes, or try the recipes in my book!

I created this book with something important in mind. I know how each family seems to have at least one picky eater or someone with special dietary needs. No problem. Just swap out one menu item for another. It's also my hope that these recipes will help that picky eater of yours explore new flavors and textures.

Take inspiration from the change of seasons, cold and cozy nights, neighbors stopping by for a drink, or a fun picnic in the park. Think of fun themes, special events, or holidays. You can keep things simple or go all-out extravagant. Explore not only with foods, but also with plates, bowls, and serving utensils. Be an artist and use every element to create your own work of art on the board!

THE BIG BOARD

I use several sizes of boards, from small (serves 4) to extra-large (serves 12 or more). We only use dinner boards with a lip or raised edge because food will inevitably fall off of a flat board, creating an unnecessary mess. And this is really important for family boards, where little ones are so eager to eat that food anywhere.

After many years of using a mix of boards, I finally teamed up with the craftspeople at JK Adams in Vermont to make my own line of boards. Each is food-safe, is made with beautiful lightweight woods, has attractive and easy-to-find handles, and is light enough to carry anywhere.

Here are other features to look for in a dinner board:

- Make sure the board is food-safe (or else you will need to lay down parchment paper). If you have a food-safe board, there is typically very little board maintenance, except to wash with soapy water, rinse, and towel dry at the end of the meal.

- Make sure you can lift or carry the board not just to a dinner table, but also outside, and even to your car.

My favorites sizes are:

- 20-inch (51-cm) round

- 26-inch (66-cm) round

- 12 x 36-inch (30 x 76-cm) rectangular

- 23-inch (58-cm) lazy Susan

BIG BOARD ESSENTIALS

I use the same bowls and tongs over and over. It's actually quite simple and fun to focus on the food, and not worry as much about the accessories. This is what I keep on hand:

- Hot pads (essential if you are serving something hot, as you do not want to scorch your board) or trivets

- Small and medium-size tongs

- Salad servers and serving spoons

- Knives and spreaders

- A variety of bowls between 2 and 6 inches (5 and 15 cm) wide, for sauces, dips, and condiments (a nesting bowl set is well worth the investment because it offers many sizes)

- Use what you have in dinner plates, platters, baking pans, casserole dishes, or pots

EASY, TIME-SAVING TIPS
FIND YOUR INSPIRATION

- Think about your board creation the way an artist approaches a blank canvas. Consider what will be the focal point, as well as colors that pop in the right places.

- Serve a favorite family recipe and talk about why it's so important to you. Tell your kids about the history of the recipe and why it's so important to you—chances are it will be their first time learning about your special story.

- Look to the changing seasons, inspired by colors, tastes, and seasonal foods, which are often found at your local farmers' market.

- Let special events be a guide—think bridal and baby showers, tailgating, picnicking, camping, backyard barbecues, pool parties, birthdays, achievement celebrations, holidays, and more.

- Explore different parts of the world and culinary dishes with your family. Read or watch shows about each country while feasting on its cuisine. Not only will you discover new ingredients and dishes, but also you'll better understand food's connection to culture.

- For multigenerational gatherings, invite grandparents, aunts and uncles, or elderly neighbors over to enjoy a board.

- You're inspired by boards, but not the cooking process? That's okay, because with boards you can find almost everything in your local deli, bakery, or farmers' market.

SIMPLE STEPS TO MAKING YOUR CREATION

1. Plan your menu by writing down the recipes or taking a picture of the ones in this book.

2. Search your pantry before you go shopping. You might already have some of the ingredients, or substitute with something similar, saving your family money and time.

3. Know how many people you are serving; scale the size of the board to the number you are feeding.

4. Decide which ingredients or main dish will be the "star" of your board.

5. When you're short on time, take shortcuts. Buy a rotisserie chicken, brownies at the bakery, or potato salad at the deli. Not everything needs to be from scratch.

6. If guests are coming over, ask them to bring an aspect, or "wedge," for the board. You might think this is a burden, but it's not. We've seen how people love to contribute.

7. Prep as much as you can in advance. For example, you can make the main dish ahead of time and assemble the board an hour before serving.

PUT IT ALL TOGETHER

1. Start with your focal point, then build around it. Place what you will be serving as your main dish in a 9 x 13-inch (23 x 33-cm) pan, dinner plate, or casserole dish; this holds the space so you can see the vision of the board and how to best assemble food around it. Always use a hot pad or trivet when setting a hot dish on a food board.

2. Do you want to create a design? Play with the shapes and lines of your ingredients and dishes—make them straight, spiraled, diagonal, triangular, or spontaneous!

3. Next, fill any small bowls with dips, spreads, jams, condiments, or sauces.

4. Fill in the remaining part of the board with seasonal produce, fresh herbs, crackers, chips, and nuts—or simply leave empty spaces.

5. Always plate the hot food last, right before serving the board. Keep the extra food warm in the oven and replenish when needed.

6. If you plan to have refills for perishable foods, keep them stocked in the fridge and refill as needed.

7. Set out the dishes you will need for serving, with utensils and plenty of napkins.

THE EXTRAS

For a fun night, take it a step further and plan on a family game, charades, or some snappy conversation starters. Or how about eating and watching a movie together? Serve a board outside or bring it along on a picnic.

Simple conversation starters:

- What is your middle name and how did you get it?

- What is the first concert you attended?

- What was your favorite part of the day?

- What subject do you enjoy the most and least in school and why?

- What job do you see yourself having when you grow up?

- Share a story about your kids when they were babies or toddlers.

- Share what your life was like when you were your kids' ages.

- What is your favorite meal that mom cooks? What about dad? (This is a fun one and can lead to some future board ideas!)

- What is the one food that you will not eat and why?

- Who is your favorite family member outside of this family?

- Five years from now, what do you think you'll be doing?

- What is your favorite app on your phone and why?

- What is your favorite movie and why?

MAGIC AROUND THE BOARD

A board is a creation of love that you make for your family or loved ones, because in a unique way, those who feed people lead people. It doesn't have to be perfect, and ingredients can vary from board to board. Make it your own, use what you have, and don't take it too seriously. The goal is to bring people together in a casual setting, in a unique way.

I like to think about the sweet moments when I created a great board for family or friends, and the looks on their faces when they saw the board for the first time. The smile on their faces, and the look in their eyes, is more than surprise—it's also about being loved, honored, and cherished. I'm honored to be a part of your family board and table!

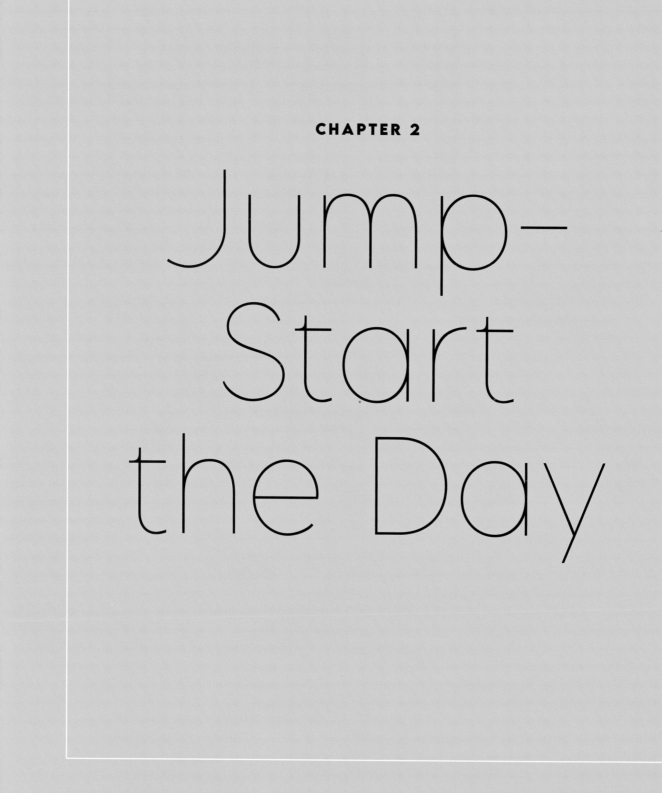

CHAPTER 2

Jump-Start the Day

The breakfast table is where the morning light meets the best light within us, where our thoughts and intentions are most earnest, honest, and caring—and something that important shouldn't be rushed!

Set the stage for meaningful connections and a leisurely morning meal with a Steel-Cut Oats Board, a Weekend Breakfast Taco Board, or a European Breakfast Charcuterie Board (pretend you're across the pond).

Get the conversational ball rolling with fun questions, such as: What was your favorite breakfast in another country or what was your favorite camping breakfast? After sharing a good meal, you'll be nourished and ready to seize the day!

STEEL-CUT OATS BOARD

Steel-cut oats are an inexpensive, filling, and a delicious wonder that can be savory or sweet. You can add in seasonal fruits and spice it up with a teaspoon of cinnamon and a pinch of nutmeg. Or you can add bacon, a sunny-side-up egg, and some red pepper flakes for a savory twist. If you have the time, toast your oats to add a warm, nutty flavor to your dish! Here's a pro tip: Cook your oats in a cast-iron pot to help keep them warm for a longer period of time.

FOR THE BOARD:

20-inch (51-cm) food board

Steel-Cut Oats (recipe follows)

¾ cup (110 g) toasted walnuts

¾ cup (90 g) sliced almonds

¾ cup (110 g) toasted pecans

⅓ cup (115 g) honey

⅓ cup (80 g) Nutella

⅓ cup (80 g) almond butter

2 bananas

1 apple, cored

Lemon juice

1 orange

½ cup (70 g) roasted pepitas

½ cup (75 g) dried cherries

½ cup (65 g) dried apricots

1 ½ cups (225 g) fresh raspberries

2 cups (300 g) strawberries

1 ½ cups (225 g) blueberries

Edible flowers, for garnish (optional)

FOR THE STEEL-CUT OATS:

¼ cup (60 g) unsalted butter

2 cups (160 g) quick cooking steel-cut oats (if steel-cut oats are not quick cooking, cook according to package instructions)

2 ½ cups (600 ml) water

1 ½ cups (360 ml) milk (dairy or nondairy)

Pinch of salt

1 teaspoon vanilla extract (optional)

BOARD ASSEMBLY:

1. Set a hot pad in the center of the board where the pot of steel-cut oats will be placed.

2. Fill 3 bowls with the walnuts, almonds, and pecans. Fill 3 smaller bowls with honey, Nutella, and almond butter. Arrange around the outside of where the oats will be placed.

3. Slice the bananas and apple and drizzle with lemon juice to prevent browning. Fan around the outer edge of the board.

4. Cut the orange into wedges, and place on the outside of the board. Fill in open areas with the pepitas, dried cherries, apricots, raspberries, strawberries, and blueberries.

5. Set the pot of oats on the hot pad and keep covered until right before serving. Garnish with edible flowers, if using.

STEEL-CUT OATS:

1. In a large skillet, heat the butter over medium heat. Add the dry oats and toast for 4 minutes, until nutty and fragrant. Set aside.

2. In a saucepan, combine the water and milk and bring to a simmer. Add the toasted oats, a pinch of salt, and the vanilla. Cook over medium heat, stirring occasionally, for 15 to 20 minutes, or until oats are thickened and creamy. Allow the oats to cool for 5 minutes before serving.

YIELD: 6 or more servings

TEA PARTY BRUNCH BOARD

When I visited Downton Abbey a few years ago, I was lucky enough to have tea with Lady Carnarvon at Highclere Castle. The experience was unforgettable, especially the tea cakes. When I came home, I immediately made my own lavender bread recipe and a board to go with it. The bread is accompanied by other tea party regulars, like delicate open-faced tea sandwiches, madeleines, scones, and of course, hot tea. Don't forget the cream and sugar!

FOR THE BOARD:

26-inch (66-cm) food board

Downton Abbey Lavender Tea Bread (recipe follows)

12 Smoked Salmon Cucumber Sandwiches (see Tip)

10 Ham and Rye Sandwiches (see Tip)

½ cup (120 g) clotted cream

½ cup (120 g) lemon curd

8 chocolate almond biscotti

10 madeleines

3 cups (450 g) blueberries

6 mini orange cranberry scones

1-pound (454 g) strawberries

6 mini blueberry tea scones

12 shortbread cookies

FOR THE DOWNTON ABBEY LAVENDER TEA BREAD:

¾ cup (180 ml) milk

1 tablespoon (5 g) culinary-grade fresh lavender, finely chopped (or 3 to 4 teaspoons dried)

6 tablespoons (90 g) unsalted butter, softened

1 cup (200 g) granulated sugar

2 eggs

¼ cup (60 g) Greek yogurt, plain or vanilla

1 teaspoon lemon zest

1 teaspoon vanilla extract, divided

BOARD ASSEMBLY:

1. On a large board, place 2 large plates, with the tea sandwiches, on each side.

2. Slice the lavender tea bread and fan into an "S" shape down the center of the board.

3. Fill 2 small bowls with clotted cream and lemon curd. Arrange all the items on the board as desired.

4. Serve with your favorite tea!

DOWNTON ABBEY LAVENDER TEA BREAD:

1. Preheat the oven to 325°F (170°C, or gas mark 3). Grease and flour one 9 x 5-inch (23 x 13-cm) loaf pan or three 3 ½ x 6-inch (9 x 15-cm) mini loaf pans.

2. Combine the milk and lavender in a small saucepan over medium heat. Heat to a simmer, then remove from the heat, and allow to cool slightly.

3. In a medium mixing bowl with a hand mixer, cream together the butter and granulated sugar until smooth. Beat in the eggs until the mixture is light and fluffy; add the Greek yogurt, lemon zest, and ½ teaspoon of the vanilla.

4. In a separate bowl, combine the flour, baking powder, and salt; gently blend into the creamed mixture, alternating with the milk and lavender, until just blended. Pour the batter into the prepared pan(s).

5. Bake for 45 to 50 minutes in the standard loaf pan or 30 minutes in the mini loaf pans.

(CONTINUED)

2 cups (240 g) all-purpose flour

1 ½ teaspoons baking powder

½ teaspoon salt

⅔ cup (80 g) sifted powdered sugar

1 tablespoon (15 ml) lemon juice

6. In a separate bowl, combine the powdered sugar, lemon juice, and remaining ½ teaspoon vanilla. Poke holes with a fork into each loaf (about 6 to 8 times per loaf). Spread the glaze over the hot cake(s). Cool in the pan for 20 minutes on a wire rack, then remove each loaf from the pan. Cool completely on a wire rack.

YIELD: 8 or more servings

TIP: For the Smoked Salmon Cucumber Sandwiches: 12 slices white bread, 6 ounces (168 g) cream cheese, 12 thin slices English cucumber, 12 ounces (336 g) smoked salmon, chopped fresh dill (garnish). Using a 3-inch (7.5-cm) round cookie or biscuit cutter, cut out circles from the bread. Spread with ½ ounce (14 g) cream cheese, then top with a cucumber slice and ½-ounce (14 g) smoked salmon; garnish with fresh dill. Make ahead and refrigerate.

TIP: For the Ham and Rye Sandwiches: 5 slices rye bread, 10 teaspoons (50 ml) honey Dijon mustard, 5 ounces (140 g) thinly sliced ham. Using a 3-inch (7.5-cm round cookie or biscuit cutter, cut out 2 circles from each slice of bread. Spread each circle with 1 teaspoon honey Dijon mustard and top with ½ ounce (14 g) ham. Make ahead and refrigerate.

CROQUE MADAME–STUFFED CROISSANT BOARD

One afternoon my daughter, Abby, was daydreaming about food, as she often does. She had an idea about how to make the already delicious croque madame even better: stuff its contents into a croissant. And thus, the croque madame–stuffed croissant was born. The recipe requires time and care to make the béchamel sauce and gently cooked scrambled eggs, but I assure you it is well worth it! Make the béchamel sauce and the croque madames first, then assemble the board while the sandwiches are baking.

FOR THE BOARD:

20-inch (51-cm) food board

Cheesy Béchamel Sauce (recipe follows)

Croque Madame–Stuffed Croissants (recipe follows)

4 eclairs

3 macarons

8 danish

3 cups (450 g) green grapes

2 cups (300 g) red grapes

1 red Anjou pear, cored and sliced just before serving

1 peach, pitted and sliced just before serving

Fresh basil, for garnish

FOR THE CHEESY BÉCHAMEL SAUCE:

¼ cup (60 g) unsalted butter

¼ cup (30 g) unbleached flour

2 ½ cups (600 ml) whole milk, warmed

1 teaspoon salt, plus more to taste

Generous pinch of nutmeg

2 tablespoons (30 g) Dijon mustard

¾ cup (90 g) grated Gruyère cheese

BOARD ASSEMBLY:

1. On a board, lay down a hot pad and a 9 x 13-inch (23 x 33-cm) pan to put the sandwiches on when they are done baking.

2. Arrange all the items on the board as desired.

3. When the main dish is baked and ready for serving, place it on the board.

4. Garnish with the basil.

CHEESY BÉCHAMEL SAUCE:

1. In a heavy-bottomed saucepan, melt the butter over medium-low heat. Add the flour and whisk for 2 minutes to form a paste. Stream in the warmed milk a little at a time, stirring constantly, until the sauce is smooth.

2. Bring the sauce to a boil and stir in the salt and nutmeg, then reduce the heat and cook for 2 minutes more. The sauce should be thick enough to coat the back of a spoon. Stir in the mustard and cheese.

3. Stir until smooth, then press a sheet of wax paper directly on top of the sauce until ready to use.

(CONTINUED)

FOR THE CROQUE MADAME–STUFFED CROISSANTS:

6 large, plain croissants

8 eggs

¾ teaspoon kosher salt

3 tablespoons (45 g) unsalted butter or olive oil

6 pieces thinly sliced ham

¾ cup (90 g) grated Gruyère cheese

CROQUE MADAME–STUFFED CROISSANTS:

1. Preheat the oven to 375°F (190°C, or gas mark 5) and lightly grease the bottom of a 9 x 13-inch (23 x 33-cm) baking dish with nonstick spray.

2. Using a small, sharp knife, make a 3-inch (7.5-cm) deep incision lengthwise into the center of each croissant to create a pocket that divides the top from the bottom, but do not cut all the way through. Set aside.

3. In a medium-size mixing bowl, whisk the eggs with the salt.

4. In a 10-inch (25-cm) nonstick skillet, melt the butter over low heat. Add the eggs, stirring frequently to create small curds—aim to undercook the eggs so they do not overcook in the oven. When the eggs are thickened but still glossy, transfer to a bowl and set aside.

5. Spoon ¼ heaping cup (60 ml) of béchamel into the bottom of the prepared pan. Place the croissants, lengthwise and slit side up, in the pan in two rows of three.

6. Spoon about 2 heaping tablespoons (30 ml) of béchamel into each croissant, followed by a folded piece of ham and one-sixth of the scrambled eggs. Repeat for all 6 croissants.

7. Top the croissants with the remaining béchamel—try to spread the sauce onto the entire croissant, even the outside, to prevent burning. Sprinkle with the cheese and cover with a sheet of parchment followed by foil.

8. Bake for 20 minutes on the center rack, covered, then for 10 to 12 min uncovered, or until the cheese starts to brown. Finish off the croissants by broiling them under high heat for 1 to 2 minutes. Serve warm.

YIELD: 6 or more servings

EUROPEAN BREAKFAST CHARCUTERIE BOARD

It is said that breakfast is the most important meal of the day. It's the meal that encourages eating savory *and* sweet noshes simultaneously, and this is especially true in European countries. This board includes some of my favorite European breakfast goodies: croissants, delicate pastries, thinly sliced meats and cheeses, fresh orange juice, creamy Nutella, jammy eggs, and more.

FOR THE BOARD:

28-inch (71-cm) food board

8 brats, cooked and kept warm

10 slices bacon, cooked and kept warm

8 croissants

8 scones, variety

1 small baguette, sliced if desired

2 tablespoons (30 g) unsalted butter 8 ounces (224 g) ham, thinly sliced

4 ounces (112 g) Cheddar cheese, sliced

4 ounces (112 g) Swiss cheese, sliced

8 ounces (224 g) smoked sockeye salmon

¼ cup (60 g) strawberry jam

¼ cup (60 g) apricot jam

¼ cup (60 g) lemon curd

½ cup (120 g) Nutella

6 soft-boiled eggs, peeled

1 tablespoon (2 g) chopped chives

8 ounces (227 g) Brie triple crème wedge

6 ounces (168 g) salami

3 ½ ounces (100 g) prosciutto

6 tomatoes, halved

1 cup (150 g) fresh blueberries

6 slices cantaloupe

1 blood orange, sliced

2 cups (300 g) red grapes

Basil, for garnish

Orange juice

BOARD ASSEMBLY:

1. On a large board, place a plate off to the side (about 9 inches, or 23 cm) to hold the cooked brats and bacon. Set a hot pad under the plate.

2. On the left side, arrange the croissant. In front of them, lay down the scones. Across from the croissants lay down the baguette with a small dish of butter (optional to slice or leave whole).

3. Roll the ham into slender rolls and arrange with the sliced cheese (every other piece Cheddar, and then Swiss), along with a row of sockeye salmon.

4. Fill 4 small bowls with the jams, lemon curd, and Nutella. Arrange on the board.

5. Cut the soft-boiled eggs in half, if desired, and place in the center of the board. Garnish with the fresh chopped chives.

6. Lay down the block of cheese, placing the salami and prosciutto around it.

7. Fill open areas with the tomatoes, blueberries, cantaloupe, blood orange slices, and grapes.

8. Right before serving, fill the empty plate with the warmed brats and bacon. Garnish the board with fresh basil. Serve with fresh-squeezed orange juice.

YIELD: 12 servings

WEEKEND BREAKFAST TACO BOARD

Crispy potatoes, cheesy eggs, hints of sweet onion, and spicy chorizo perfectly meld together when wrapped in a steamed corn tortilla. Often, potato chorizo breakfast hash calls for cracking whole eggs onto the potatoes and steaming or baking in the oven until the eggs are set. This can be messy, which is why I scramble the eggs for easy serving—no dripping yolks or unset egg whites in these tacos! This breakfast is sure to satisfy your family and friends, so give it a try.

FOR THE BOARD:

26-inch (66-cm) food board

Chorizo Potato Breakfast Hash (recipe follows)

2 packages (12 ounces, or 336 g) corn tortillas, warmed

1 cup (150 g) cherry tomatoes, halved

½ cup (120 g) sour cream

½ cup (8 g) chopped cilantro, plus extra for garnish

2 jalapeño peppers, sliced

1 ½ cups (225 g) corn, drained

2 cups (480 g) guacamole

1 cup (240 ml) salsa

3 cups (150 g) tortilla chips

1 cup (70 g) thinly sliced red cabbage

1 pound (454 g) pineapple chunks

1 pound (454 g) watermelon chunks

1 pound (454 g) cantaloupe chunks

1 pound (454 g) honeydew melon chunks

BOARD ASSEMBLY:

1. On a large board, place two stacked hot pads or a trivet in the center for the skillet. (The skillet will be very hot.) Place the warm tortillas in a linen towel or a basket, and place on the inside edge of the board.

2. Fill 7 small bowls with the tomatoes, sour cream, cilantro, jalapeño, corn, guacamole, and salsa, and place on the board. Fill in empty spaces with the chips. Next, lay down the cabbage.

3. Arrange the pineapple, watermelon, cantaloupe, and honeydew melon on the board.

4. When ready to serve, set the skillet of chorizo hash on the board. FIESTA!

FOR THE CHORIZO POTATO BREAKFAST HASH:

2 pounds (908 g) Yukon Gold potatoes, cut into ½-inch (1.3-cm) pieces

2 ½ tablespoons (37 ml) apple cider vinegar

2 tablespoons (30 g) kosher salt, plus more to taste

¼ cup (60 ml) avocado or canola oil, divided

1 pound (454 g) ground chorizo, removed from casing

4 strips maple center-cut bacon, cut into 1-inch (2.5-cm) pieces

1 yellow onion, diced

4 cloves garlic, minced

1 teaspoon coriander

1 teaspoon cumin

¾ teaspoon smoked paprika

Freshly ground black pepper

10 eggs, beaten

6 slices sharp yellow Cheddar cheese

½ cup (8 g) chopped cilantro

CHORIZO POTATO BREAKFAST HASH:

1. Preheat the oven to 375°F (190°C, or gas mark 5).

2. Place the potatoes in a large saucepan and cover with 6 cups (1440 ml) cold water, the apple cider vinegar, and the salt; stir. Bring the water to a boil, then reduce to a simmer. Simmer for 6 to 8 minutes, until the potatoes are fork tender. Drain the potatoes and set aside.

3. In a 12-inch (30-cm) cast-iron skillet, heat 1 tablespoon (15 ml) of the oil over medium heat. When the oil is hot, add the chorizo and bacon. Cook for 8 to 10 minutes.

4. Remove the chorizo and bacon, leaving the fat in the skillet, and transfer to a plate. Add the onion and garlic to the skillet and cook over medium-low heat until tender, 10 to 12 minutes. Transfer the onions to the plate with the meat.

5. Heat 2 tablespoons (45 ml) oil in the skillet over medium-high heat. Add the potatoes and cook, stirring occasionally, until browned and crisp, 20 minutes or so. Add the coriander, cumin, and paprika and stir to coat. Add salt and pepper to taste; add the meat mixture to the potatoes, stir to combine, and set aside.

6. In a medium nonstick skillet, heat the remaining 1 tablespoon (15 ml) oil over medium heat. Add the beaten eggs and season with salt; cook the eggs until just scrambled—don't overcook.

7. Transfer the eggs to the top of the hash and top with the Cheddar slices. Cover with a lid or foil to melt the cheese. Garnish the top with the chopped cilantro. Keep warm until serving.

YIELD: 8 or more servings

MEDITERRANEAN SHAKSHUKA BOARD

Shakshuka is often served for dinner at my house—breakfast for dinner is a big theme in my life. It is easy to make, deliciously rich in flavor, and incredibly comforting. For these reasons, it also makes a perfect breakfast meal, especially when served with warm hummus and tangy labneh. Enjoy this shakshuka board for any meal of the day, and don't forget the flatbread—I recommend ordering fresh naan, pita, or other flatbread from your local Mediterranean or Middle Eastern restaurant.

FOR THE BOARD:

24 to 26-inch (60–66 cm) food board

Mediterranean Cucumber Tomato Salad (see Tip, or buy from local deli)

Mediterranean Shakshuka (recipe follows)

8 ounces (224 g) hummus

6 ounces (168 g) labneh

¾ cup (120 g) plus 2 tablespoons (20 g) kalamata olives, divided

6 to 8 whole mint leaves plus 2 tablespoons (6 g) chopped mint, divided

Olive oil, for drizzling

2 tablespoons (12 g) dukkah (optional)

3 large garlic naan or other flatbread, cut into large triangles

Parsley sprigs, for garnish

Mint sprigs, for garnish

BOARD ASSEMBLY:

1. Place a hot pad or trivet on the board to hold the shakshuka. Place the Mediterranean Cucumber Tomato Salad in a medium bowl; refrigerate. Make the Mediterranean Shakshuka, and while baking, prepare the board.

2. Spread the hummus in a 1-inch (2.5-cm) layer on one plate, and the labneh on another. Sprinkle the hummus with 2 tablespoons (20 g) of the olives, the whole mint leaves, and a drizzle of olive oil. Garnish the labneh with the dukkah, chopped mint, and a drizzle of olive oil. Place on the board.

3. Fill a small bowl with the remaining ¾ cup (120 g) olives and place on the board. Add the Mediterranean salad to the board.

4. Fill in any remaining space with the pita bread triangles. Garnish the board with sprigs of parsley around the bowl of olives, and mint sprigs tucked in around the naan bread.

5. Place the shakshuka on the board, keeping the lid on until ready to serve.

FOR THE MEDITERRANEAN SHAKSHUKA:

3 tablespoons (45 ml) olive oil

1 yellow onion, diced

2 jalapeños, diced

1 large red bell pepper, seeded and finely diced

1 teaspoon kosher salt, divided, plus more to taste

8 cloves garlic, crushed

2 teaspoons (10 g) tomato paste

1 teaspoon cumin

2 teaspoons (16 g) smoked paprika

½ teaspoon black pepper

1 cup (240 ml) vegetable or chicken broth

1 can (28 ounces, or 785 g) whole peeled tomatoes

1 cup (150 g) crumbled feta cheese, divided

8 eggs

¼ cup (16 g) chopped parsley

2 tablespoons (8 g) chopped mint

MEDITERRANEAN SHAKSHUKA:

1. Preheat the oven to 375°F (190°C, or gas mark 5).

2. In a shallow 3-quart (2.7-L) Dutch oven, heat the olive oil over medium-high heat. When the oil shimmers, add the onion, jalapeño, red bell pepper, and ½ teaspoon of the salt. Cook until tender, 20 to 23 minutes.

3. Stir in the garlic and tomato paste. Cook for 5 to 7 minutes. Mix in the cumin, smoked paprika, black pepper, and remaining ½ teaspoon salt and cook for 2 minutes.

4. Add the broth and crushed tomatoes with their juices. Stir and bring to a simmer for 15 to 20 minutes, until the tomatoes have thickened.

5. Stir in ⅔ cup (100 g) of the feta. With a spoon, create 8 shallow wells. Gently crack an egg into each.

6. Transfer the pan to the oven and bake for 7 to 10 minutes, until the eggs are set. Remove from the oven and sprinkle with the remaining ⅓ cup (50 g) feta, parsley, and mint.

YIELD: 6 or more servings

TIP: For the Mediterranean Cucumber Tomato Salad: In a large bowl, combine 1 pound (454 g) Campari tomatoes, quartered; 4 to 5 Persian cucumbers, cut into 1-inch (2.5-cm) pieces; ¼ red onion, sliced; ¼ cup (16 g) chopped parsley; ¼ cup (16 g) chopped mint; and 2 scallions, sliced. In a small bowl, whisk together the juice of 1 lemon, 2 tablespoons (30 ml) olive oil, and salt and pepper to taste. Drizzle over the veggies and gently mix. Refrigerate until ready to serve. Garnish with extra chopped parsley and mint.

SHEET-PAN BANANA PANCAKE BOARD

Take ordinary pancakes and turn them into a giant one for this fun breakfast (or dinner) board. This recipe is a fusion of a traditional pancake and an upside-down cake. Forget the syrup, as the brown sugar and butter add enough sweetness to soak into the pancakes and caramelize the bacon and bananas. And flipping the pancake upside down allows that buttery goodness to seep into the pancake. Any leftovers? Make a delicious breakfast sandwich! Oh, so good! Make the pancake first and keep warm until ready to serve.

FOR THE BOARD:

24 to 26-inch (60–66 cm) food board

Sheet-Pan Banana Pancake (recipe follows)

1 ½ tablespoons (23 ml) olive oil

12 eggs, beaten

1 ½ teaspoons kosher salt

½ cup (60 g) grated sharp Cheddar cheese

1 tablespoon (5 g) chopped scallion, for garnish

1 package (20 ounces, or 560 g) maple breakfast sausage, cooked

1 cup (240 ml) heavy cream

¼ cup (30 g) powdered sugar

½ teaspoon vanilla extract

2 pounds (908 g) strawberries

1 pound (454 g) blueberries

1 cantaloupe, cut into 2-inch (5-cm) pieces

Mint, for garnish

BOARD ASSEMBLY:

1. Place 3 hot pads or trivets on the board to hold the pancake. Place a large bowl on the board to hold the scrambled eggs and a medium bowl to hold the sausages. Place a hot pad or trivet underneath each bowl.

2. Heat the oil in a large nonstick skillet. Pour in the eggs and sprinkle with the salt and cheese. Cook, scrambling, until just set and no longer wet. Pour into the bowl, scatter the scallions on top, and cover to keep warm.

3. Cook the sausage according to package directions, place in a medium bowl, set on the board, and cover to keep warm.

4. In a bowl using a mixer, whip the cream for 2 to 3 minutes until thick; add the powdered sugar and vanilla. Gently mix, transfer a medium bowl, and place on the board.

5. Fill in the spaces with the strawberries, blueberries, and cantaloupe and small sprigs of mint.

FOR THE SHEET-PAN BANANA PANCAKE:

2 ¼ cups (540 ml) buttermilk

½ cup (120 g) Greek yogurt

2 eggs

¼ cup (60 ml) water

2 ½ teaspoons (12 ml) vanilla extract, divided

2 teaspoons (10 g) kosher salt, divided

¼ cup (50 g) granulated sugar

½ cup plus 2 tablespoons (125 g) packed dark brown sugar, divided

2 ¼ cups (270 g) all-purpose flour

1 teaspoon baking powder

1 ¼ teaspoons baking soda

1 teaspoon cinnamon

1 tablespoon (15 ml) maple syrup

¼ cup (60 g) unsalted butter

8 ounces (224 g) bacon, cooked

3 to 4 bananas, peeled and quartered

SHEET-PAN BANANA PANCAKE:

1. Preheat the oven to 500°F (250°C, or gas mark 10). Coat a 13 x 18-inch (33 x 46-cm) baking sheet with nonstick spray on the bottom and the edges (important for ensuring your pancake flips out of the pan). Place a piece of parchment on the bottom of the sheet pan and set aside.

2. In a large mixing bowl, whisk together the buttermilk, yogurt, eggs, water, 2 teaspoons (10 ml) of the vanilla, 1 ½ teaspoons (8 g) of the salt, granulated sugar, and 2 tablespoons (25 g) of the brown sugar. Set aside.

3. In a separate bowl, combine the flour, baking powder, baking soda, and cinnamon. Set aside.

4. In a small saucepan, combine the remaining ½ cup (100 g) brown sugar, remaining ½ teaspoon (2 ml) vanilla, remaining ½ teaspoon (2 g) salt, maple syrup, and butter. Cook over medium heat, stirring, until the sugar begins to bubble. Remove from the heat and spread evenly onto the parchment-lined baking sheet. Lay down the bacon and bananas on the brown sugar mixture in diagonal rows, alternating bananas and bacon.

5. Pour the flour mixture into the wet ingredients and whisk together. Small clumps are okay; do not overmix. Spread the batter over the bacon and bananas, gently smoothing the top.

6. Immediately place in the oven and reduce the temperature to 400°F (200°C, or gas mark 6). Bake for 15 to 18 minutes, or until a cake tester comes out clean and the top of the pancake is lightly browned.

7. Remove from the oven and let cool for 3 to 4 minutes. Using a sharp knife, carefully cut around the edges to ensure the pancake releases. Flip the pan upside down onto a large platter or cutting board. Remove the pan and gently pull the parchment off. Cut the pancake into squares, arrange on a platter, and keep warm until ready to serve, then place on the board.

YIELD: 8 or more servings

CHINESE CONGEE BOARD

Porridge variations are found across all cultural cuisines. Here on the West Coast of the United States, I grew up eating oatmeal with brown sugar, raisins, and cream, and so did my kids. Now that we have a new family member, Vicky, my Chinese daughter-in-law (who is an excellent cook), I wanted to learn about dishes she grew up eating. She shared her culture's version of porridge with us: congee, a simple rice porridge with many variations, both savory and sweet. To be honest, I find it to be much more satisfying than oatmeal, especially when served with steamed buns and delicious dumplings. Thanks for the inspiration, Vicky!

FOR THE BOARD:

24 to 26-inch (60–66 cm) food board

Congee (recipe follows)
    2 cups (280 g) shredded chicken, cooked shrimp, or marinated pork

3 soft-boiled eggs

3 soft-boiled preserved duck eggs (or more soft-boiled eggs if you can't find preserved duck eggs)

¼ cup (60 ml) chili crisp or chili oil

2 green onion buns

3 barbecue pork dumplings

4 pork shumai

10 shrimp dumplings

6 Chinese donuts

6 sesame mochi balls

4 egg tarts

2 red bean mochi

3 chicken curry buns

BOARD ASSEMBLY:

1. On a large board, place 2 hot pads or trivets, and place 2 large bowls on opposite sides (to hold the hot congee).

2. Place the shredded chicken in one bowl and all the soft-boiled eggs in another bowl and place on the board. In a small bowl, add the chili crisp.

3. Around the inside edge, place the green onion buns, pork dumplings, shumai, shrimp dumplings, and 3 stacked soup spoons. Along the other inside edge, place the Chinese donuts, sesame mochi balls, egg tarts, and red bean mochi. Place the chicken curry buns along the lip of the board.

4. Lastly, pour the congee into the 2 large bowls.

FOR THE CONGEE:

8 cups (1920 ml) water

1 tablespoon (8 g) vegetable or chicken bouillon (or 8 cups [1920 ml] premade broth)

1 cup (165 g) long-grain rice, rinsed

3 tablespoons (45 ml) peanut oil or other oil with a high smoke point, divided

10 ounces (280 g) enoki mushrooms

Salt to taste

8 ounces (224 g) shiitake mushrooms

4 baby bok choy, stalks cut into 1-inch (2.5-cm) pieces, leaves reserved

1- to 2-inch (2.5- to 5-cm) piece fresh ginger, peeled and cut into matchsticks

4 scallions, thinly sliced, plus more to garnish

2 to 3 tablespoons (16 to 24 g) roasted peanuts, roughly chopped, plus more for garnish

CONGEE:

1. In a 3-quart (2.7-L) pot, heat the water over medium heat, add the bouillon, and stir until dissolved. Add the rice, bring the liquid to a boil over high heat, then reduce to a simmer and partially cover with a lid. Stir the congee occasionally for an hour. Continue stirring more frequently, for an additional ½ hour, as the congee thickens.

2. Heat 1 tablespoon (15 ml) of the peanut oil in a large skillet over medium-high heat. When the oil is hot, add the enoki mushrooms in a single layer and toss in the oil. Allow the mushrooms to sit, undisturbed, for 3 minutes until lightly brown. Reduce the heat to medium and continue cooking, adding salt to taste and stirring occasionally, until they release their liquid, 5 to 7 more minutes depending on thickness. Repeat for the shiitake mushrooms. Set the mushrooms aside and keep warm.

3. Heat the remaining 2 tablespoons (30 ml) peanut oil over medium-high heat in a large skillet. When hot, add the bok choy stalks (reserve the leaves for later), ginger, and a pinch of salt. Cook, stirring occasionally, until the stalks soften, 2 to 3 minutes. Add the bok choy leaves and scallion. Cook for another 1 to 2 minutes, then remove from the heat and add to the congee during the last half hour of simmering. Garnish with the peanuts and scallion.

YIELD: 6 or more servings

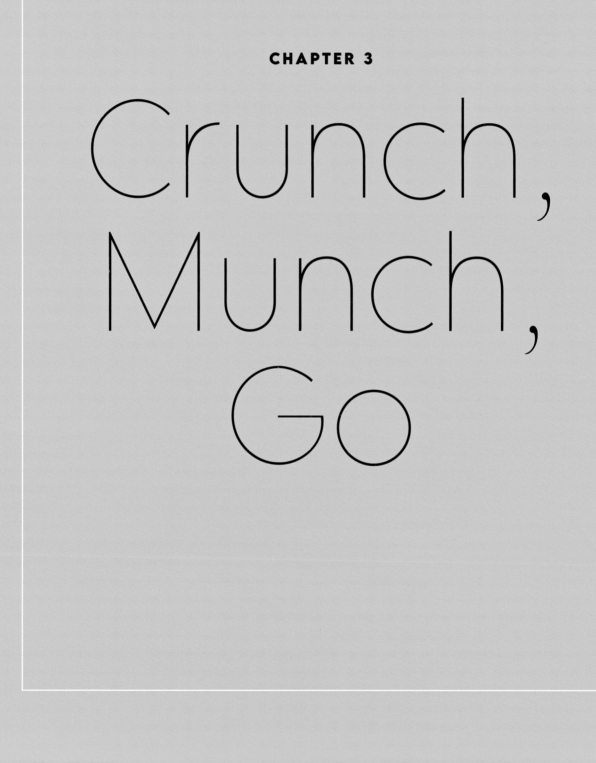

CHAPTER 3

Crunch, Munch, Go

Snacks don't have to be fancy. They just have to be wholesome, tasty, and fun to eat.

Clean out the fridge to make fruit and veggies skewers with your favorite dip or make wholesome energy balls that you keep in the freezer and pull out for the After-School Energy Bites Board. Snack boards are quick to make and a great way to get kids in the kitchen! They'll love the Make-Your-Own Taco Cups Board or Mini Club Sandwich Kebabs Board. Inspire their creativity by showing them how to make roll-ups with their favorite veggies in the Veggie Roll-Up Snack Board! Can't think of anything new? That's okay, because you can't go wrong with the classic PB&J Snack Board!

AFTER-SCHOOL ENERGY BITES BOARD

Kids of all ages love these energy bites. They are packed with fiber and healthy fats, which makes them the perfect afternoon snack to fuel you or your kids until dinner. They can be refrigerated, but make sure to let them come to room temperature before serving. Delicious to keep on hand for any "littles" who might stop by, they can also be served with some 4-inch (10-cm) veggie and fruit kebabs.

FOR THE BOARD:

15-inch (38-cm) food board

Almond Butter, Chocolate, and Cherry Energy Bites (recipe follows)

½ cup (120 ml) ranch dressing

Ten 4-inch (10-cm) kebab sticks

5 green grapes

5 strawberries

5 mango chunks

5 blueberries

5 slices green apple

5 chunks red apple

5 broccoli florets

5 cherry tomatoes

5 red pepper chunks

5 orange pepper chunks

5 baby carrots

5 radishes

FOR THE ALMOND BUTTER, CHOCOLATE, AND CHERRY ENERGY BITES:

1 cup (80 g) quick-cooking oats

¼ cup (30 g) ground flaxseed

1 cup (80 g) unsweetened shredded coconut

¾ teaspoon vanilla extract

¾ cup (180 g) creamy almond butter

⅓ teaspoon kosher salt, plus more to taste

⅓ cup (50 g) unsalted roasted sunflower seeds

3 tablespoons (45 ml) honey

3 tablespoons (45 ml) hot water

½ cup (80 g) semisweet chocolate chunks

½ cup (75 g) dried tart cherries

BOARD ASSEMBLY:

1. On the board, arrange the energy bites.

2. Place a bowl with the ranch dressing to one side.

3. Make skewers with the kebab sticks by alternating one of each fruit on 5 sticks. Do the same with the veggies on the remaining 5 sticks. Prop them up along the outer lip of the board, with the veggie kebabs next to the dressing.

ALMOND BUTTER, CHOCOLATE, AND CHERRY ENERGY BITES:

1. In a large bowl, combine the oats, flax, coconut, vanilla, almond butter, salt, sunflower seeds, honey, and hot water. Mix thoroughly until combined, then allow to rest for 15 minutes before adding the chocolate chips and cherries.

2. Divide the mixture into 10 large energy bites, about 2 inches (5 cm) thick, or alternatively, divide into 20 smaller bites.

3. Refrigerate the bites until ready to serve. Remove from the refrigerator an hour or so in advance to ensure they come to room temperature before serving.

YIELD: 5 or more servings

MINI CLUB SANDWICH KEBABS BOARD

Here's a kid-friendly snack, both to eat and to make. Little hands are perfect for stringing food onto a skewer. For kids who don't normally like tomatoes or pickles, they just might be tempted to eat them when they're on a kebab. Set out the ingredients and let the kids make their own sandwich kebab. Like any sandwich, you can use whichever breads, meats, cheese, and veggies you prefer, in any order. You can prepare any kind of sandwich this way. Start stacking away!

FOR THE BOARD:

20-inch (51-cm) food board

⅓ cup (80 g) yellow mustard

½ cup (120 ml) ranch dressing

3 ounces (84 g) turkey, thinly sliced

3 ounces (84 g) ham, thinly sliced

1 loaf French bread, cut into 1-inch (2.5-cm) pieces

3 ounces (84 g) Cheddar cheese, cut into 1-inch (2.5-cm) cubes

3 ounces (84 g) Havarti cheese, cut into 1-inch (2.5-cm) cubes

14 grape tomatoes, various colors

14 cornichons, drained

¼ head iceberg lettuce, cut or folded into 1-inch (2.5-cm) chunks

Fourteen 6-inch (15-cm) skewers

1 pound (454 g) fresh fruit, such as strawberries

45 mini chocolate chip cookies

2 cups (100 g) potato chips

Edible flowers, for garnish (optional)

BOARD ASSEMBLY:

1. Place 2 small bowls on the board and pour the mustard into one and the ranch dressing into the other.

2. Fold the lunch meats into quarters. Thread the lunch meats, bread, cheeses, tomatoes, pickles, and lettuce onto the skewers.

3. Arrange the kebabs on the board along with the fresh fruit, cookies, and chips. If desired, add edible flowers on top and around the kebabs for garnish. Serve immediately!

MORE KEBAB IDEAS:

French toast, bacon, hard-boiled egg half, strawberry

Dollar pancakes, Canadian bacon, pineapple chunk

Peanut butter and jelly, grapes

Olives, cheese, salami

Hot dogs, cheese, bun, watermelon

YIELD: 6 or more servings

MAKE-YOUR-OWN TACO CUPS BOARD

When my kids were young, tacos were a staple meal in our house. We mostly ate them for dinner, so I wanted to reimagine a snack-friendly version. Behold the taco cup! After baking tortillas into small bowls, kiddos can easily fill them with their favorite ingredients. Add black beans or refried beans to the board for a vegetarian option.

FOR THE BOARD:

20-inch (51-cm) food board

Twenty 2-inch (5-cm) tortilla cups (see Tip, or use store-bought)

1 cup (240 ml) salsa

4 ounces (112 g) sliced olives, drained

1 cup (240 g) guacamole

1 cup (240 g) sour cream

1 cup (120 g) grated Mexican cheese

1 cup (80 g) finely shredded purple cabbage

1 cup (30 g) shredded iceberg lettuce

2 large limes, cut into wedges

½ cup (8 g) chopped cilantro

1 pound (454 g) watermelon spears

1 jalapeño, for garnish

FOR THE BASIC TACO MEAT:

2 tablespoons (30 ml) olive oil

1 pound (454 g) ground beef (preferably 80% lean, 20% fat)

1 tablespoon (6 g) chili powder

1 teaspoon cumin

½ teaspoon garlic powder

1 teaspoon salt

1 small white onion, finely diced

1 tablespoon (15 ml) water, plus more if needed

½ cup (120 ml) tomato sauce or puree

BOARD ASSEMBLY:

1. Place a hot pad and bowl on the board for the cooked meat. Around that bowl, stack the taco cups by twos, and arrange across the board in an S shape.

2. Fill small bowls with the salsa, olives, guacamole, sour cream, and cheese and place on the board. Fill in open areas with the cabbage, lettuce, lime wedges, and cilantro, leaving a larger space for the watermelon spears. Garnish with the jalapeño pepper.

BASIC TACO MEAT:

1. In a large skillet over medium-high heat, add the olive oil. Once the oil is shimmering, add the ground beef and break into large chunks with a wooden spoon. Allow the meat to sit undisturbed for 3 minutes, or until browned. Break it up into small pieces and add the spices.

2. Remove the meat from the pan and set aside. Drain off most of the fat. Reduce the heat to medium, add the onion, and season with a generous pinch of salt. Add the water, cover with a lid, and sauté for 10 minutes, stirring every 2 minutes or so. Add more water, 1 tablespoon (15 ml) at a time, if needed.

3. Add the cooked meat and tomato sauce to the mixture and cook for 5 minutes over low heat, stirring. Transfer to the bowl on the board and serve.

YIELD: 6 lunch or 10 snack servings

(CONTINUED)

TIP: To make your own taco cups, preheat the oven to 400°F (200°C, or gas mark 6). Place twenty-four 6-inch (15-cm) tortillas in the microwave or oven and heat for 30 seconds to soften them. Gently spread 1 teaspoon of mayonnaise on the front and back of each tortilla and press them into the cups on 2 standard-size muffin tins, pushing down the bottom and pinching together the folds to make a cup. Bake for 10 to 12 minutes, or until golden brown. Let cool.

VEGGIE ROLL-UP SNACK BOARD

When my kids were little, I tried to sneak veggies into many of their meals, especially when they were going through phases of picky eating. That inspired this veggie snack board, which gives kids the option to personalize their veggie roll-ups and enjoy snacking on their own nutritious creation.

FOR THE BOARD:

20-inch (51-cm) food board

10 tortillas (mixed variety of spinach and herb, tomato basil, cilantro lime, and whole wheat)

Sun-Dried Tomato Hummus (recipe follows, or use store-bought)

½ cup (120 g) classic hummus

½ cup (120 g) basil pesto

½ cup (120 g) whipped cream cheese

1 cup (80 g) shredded carrot

8 ounces (224 g) mozzarella cheese slices

1 avocado, peeled, pitted, and sliced, sprinkled with lime juice

1 English cucumber, sliced

1 ½ cups (45 g) fresh spinach leaves

3 soft-boiled eggs, sliced

3 Roma tomatoes, sliced

½ cup (15 g) chopped mint, for garnish

1 cup (30 g) chopped parsley, for garnish

BOARD ASSEMBLY:

1. Roll the tortillas and place on the edge of the board.

2. Fill 4 small bowls with the Sun-Dried Tomato Hummus, classic hummus, pesto, and cream cheese. Place on the board.

3. Next to the tortillas, lay down the shredded carrot, mozzarella, avocado, cucumber, and spinach in a circular fashion around the outside of the board.

4. In the middle of the board, arrange the sliced eggs and tomatoes. Sprinkle with salt. Fill in any open areas with the mint and parsley.

5. To make the roll-up, diners can lay the tortilla flat and spread with hummus, pesto, or cream cheese, leaving 1 inch (2.5 cm) around the outside. Lay down favorite toppings and tightly roll. Do not overfill.

(CONTINUED)

FOR THE SUN-DRIED TOMATO HUMMUS:

1 can (15 ounces, or 420 g) chickpeas, drained

¼ cup (60 g) tahini

½ cup (120 ml) olive oil, plus more for drizzling

Juice of 2 lemons

2 teaspoons (10 g) kosher salt, plus more to taste

1 head roasted garlic (see Tip), 4 to 5 whole cloves reserved for garnish, or 2 cloves raw garlic

½ cup (100 g) sun-dried tomatoes in oil

1 tablespoon (2 g) chopped fresh parsley, for garnish (optional)

SUN-DRIED TOMATO HUMMUS:

1. In a food processor, add the chickpeas, tahini, olive oil, lemon juice, and salt and blend until smooth. If you don't want to roast your garlic, add the raw garlic to the food processor at the same time as the chickpeas.

2. Add the sun-dried tomatoes and roasted garlic to the hummus mixture and continue blending until almost smooth, leaving larger pieces for added texture if desired. Taste for salt and adjust the seasoning if needed. Drizzle with more olive oil and garnish with fresh parsley and roasted garlic cloves. Refrigerate until ready to serve, for best flavor.

YIELD: 10 servings

TIP: To roast the garlic, preheat the oven to 400°F (200°C, or gas mark 6). Remove excess paper skin from the head of garlic and cut about ½ inch (1.3 cm) off the top to expose the raw cloves. Place on a piece of foil large enough to fully cover the bulb. Drizzle with about 1 teaspoon of olive oil and a pinch of salt and cover with the foil. Roast for 25 to 30 minutes, or until the cloves can easily be squeezed out and are a golden yellow color.

PRETZEL BITES BOARD

You can easily make your own warm, chewy, mini pretzel bites at home. Gather the kids in the kitchen to make this snack from scratch for a fun activity. Grab a pound of premade pizza dough from your local market and bake the bites while you're assembling the board. You'll be ready to dip to your heart's desire in no time—enjoy the bites with all your favorite sweet and savory dips!

FOR THE BOARD:

18-inch (45-cm) food board

Pizza Dough Pretzel Bites (recipe follows)

1 recipe Peanut Butter and Honey Dip (page 65)

⅓ cup (80 g) jam

¾ cup (180 g) Orange Glaze (see Tip)

½ cup (120 g) Nutella

⅓ cup (80 g) Dijon honey mustard

¾ cup (180 g) queso

½ cup (120 ml) Two-Cheese Chive Dip (see Tip)

1 green apple, cored and sliced

4 ounces (112 g) sweet soppressata (salami)

4 ounces (112 g) sweet dry sausage

4 ounces (112 g) coppa (salami)

1 tablespoon (10 g) chopped peanuts

1 tablespoon (8 g) chopped jalapeño

Freshly cracked black pepper

1 teaspoon orange zest

FOR THE PIZZA DOUGH PRETZEL BITES:

1 egg

1 tablespoon (15 ml) water

1 pound (454 g) pizza dough (herb dough is delicious, too)

⅓ cup baking soda

1 tablespoon (15 g) Maldon flake salt or 1 teaspoon kosher salt

BOARD ASSEMBLY:

1. Place a hot pad or trivet and a dinner plate on the board; this will hold the hot pretzel bites.

2. Fill 7 bowls with the peanut butter dip, jam, orange glaze, Nutella, mustard, queso, and cheese chive dip. Place around the inside edge of the board.

3. Fan the sliced apple around two of the bowls, and then fill in open areas with the meats.

4. Sprinkle the peanuts on the peanut butter dip, the chopped jalapeño and cracked pepper on the queso dip, and the orange zest on the orange glaze.

PIZZA DOUGH PRETZEL BITES:

1. Preheat the oven to 425°F (220°C, or gas mark 7) and line a large plate with paper towels. Line a baking sheet with parchment paper.

2. Whisk together the egg and water in a small bowl to make an egg wash. Set aside.

3. Divide the dough into 4 pieces, then roll each piece into a 1-inch (2.5-cm)-thick rope. Cut each rope into six 1-inch (2.5-cm) pieces to make 24 segments. Roll each segment into a ball and set aside.

4. Bring 8 cups (2 L) water to a boil in a large pot, then add the baking soda. Carefully add the dough balls to the water and boil for about 45 seconds—they will begin to float to the surface when done. Use a slotted spoon or mesh strainer to remove the dough from the water and place on the paper towels. Pat dry, then transfer to

the prepared baking sheet. Brush all sides of the dough with the egg wash, then sprinkle each ball with a pinch of salt. Bake for 14 to 16 minutes, or until the tops are golden brown.

YIELD: 8 or more servings

TIP: For the Orange Glaze: In a medium-size bowl, combine 4 ounces (112 g) soft cream cheese, ½ cup (60 g) powdered sugar, 1 tablespoon (15 ml) heavy cream, 1 teaspoon vanilla extract, 1 teaspoon orange zest, and 1 tablespoon (15 ml) fresh orange juice.

TIP: For the Two-Cheese Chive Dip: In a medium-size bowl, combine 4 ounces (112 g) soft cream cheese, 5 ounces (140 g) goat cheese, ¼ cup (5 g) finely chopped chives, and fresh cracked pepper to taste.

PB&J SNACK BOARD

This board is an ode to the humble peanut butter and jelly sandwich, the perfect food for hiking, lunching, and midnight snacking. Growing up, my kids loved to eat PB&J, so I *had* to include this board. The sandwiches are quick and easy to make, and the tangy peanut butter and honey dip is perfect for dipping fruits and vegetables. To change things up, swap out the jelly for honey, bananas, or even Nutella!

FOR THE BOARD:

20-inch (51-cm) food board

16 slices whole wheat bread

1 cup (240 g) crunchy peanut butter

½ cup (120 g) blackberry jam

½ cup (120 g) apricot jam

Peanut Butter and Honey Dip (recipe follows)

2 bunches grapes, red and green

6 ounces (168 g) mini carrot sticks

12 to 14 strawberries

1 apple, cored, sliced, and sprinkled with lemon juice

1 blood orange, sliced

Eight 3-inch (7.5-cm) celery sticks

4 ounces (112 g) chocolate-covered pretzels

3 ounces (84 g) pretzel sticks

10 ounces (280 g) blueberries

FOR THE PEANUT BUTTER AND HONEY DIP:

½ cup (120 g) Greek yogurt

¼ cup (60 g) crunchy peanut butter

2 tablespoons (30 ml) honey

½ teaspoon vanilla extract

BOARD ASSEMBLY:

1. On 8 slices of bread, spread 2 tablespoons (30 g) crunchy peanut butter. On the other 8 slices, spread 1 tablespoon (15 g) of each jelly. Place the slices of bread together to make the sandwiches. Cut off the crusts, then cut the sandwich in half diagonally to make triangles.

2. On the board, stand up the sandwiches, short flat side down, tip up, and then long side down, tip to the side. Alternate every sandwich and make a row down the center of the board.

3. Place 2 small bowls on the board for the dip, one on either side of the sandwiches.

4. Lay down the grapes and the carrot sticks on opposite sides of the board.

5. Next, lay down strawberries and apples on opposite sides of the board.

6. Fill in open areas with the orange slices, celery sticks, chocolate-covered pretzels, pretzel sticks, and blueberries.

PEANUT BUTTER AND HONEY DIP:

1. Mix all the ingredients together in a small bowl until well combined. Divide between the 2 bowls on the board.

YIELD: 8 servings

SWEET AND SAVORY TRAIL MIX BOARD

This epic trail mix board is inspired by my life in the Pacific Northwest. I have so many fond memories of hiking with my family. The kids always looked forward to taking a break to have a snack and trail mix was always our go-to. Kick-off your hike or outdoor activity by gathering around the board so everyone can make their own trail mix.

FOR THE BOARD:

24-inch (60-cm) food board

2 cups (300 g) roasted whole almonds

2 cups (300 g) roasted whole cashews

2 cups (300 g) roasted peanuts

2 cups (300 g) roasted pecans

2 cups (300 g) roasted hazelnuts

2 cups (300 g) roasted salted pistachios

1 cup (100 g) salted plantain chips

½ cup (50 g) sesame sticks

⅓ cup (40 g) wasabi peas

⅓ cup (50 g) corn nuts

1 cup (50 g) spicy chili lime tortilla twists (or similar chip)

1 cup (20 g) freeze-dried raspberries

1 cup (20 g) freeze-dried blueberries

1 cup (165 g) white chocolate chips, divided

½ cup (100 g) mini peanut butter cups

½ cup (75 g) dried tart cherries

1 ½ cups (150 g) dark chocolate–covered pretzels

¾ cup (150 g) peanut M&M's

½ cup (50 g) whole-grain Chex cereal

8 pitted dates, whole or cut in half

¾ cup (75 g) banana chips

1 cup (200 g) granola

BOARD ASSEMBLY:

1. On a large board, arrange the nuts in pie-shaped wedges.

2. Fill in spaces with the remaining ingredients, mixing sweet and savory, with about 12 ingredients per side.

3. Serve with measuring cups for scoops and small bags or jars so everyone make their own trail mix.

YIELD: 12 or more servings

CHAPTER 4

Let's Do Lunch

Too often, lunch time feels rushed and overlooked, especially on hectic days when your schedule is packed. Preparing a lunch board, even if just once a week, is the perfect opportunity to breathe and take in the day before it flies by. Slowing to down to eat, reconnect, recharge, and give your mind a break from the stress of the day is a beautiful gift you can give yourself and your family.

Serve up comfort in a bowl with Grilled Cheese and Orange Basil Tomato Soup Board, an Italian Tortellini Salad Board (kids love to pick out their favorite ingredients), or a Family-Size Nacho Board, where everyone adds their favorite toppings. While you're at it, serve up some conversation starters by asking everyone what the best part of their day has been so far.

Let's do lunch, and let's make it special!

EASY CHICKEN TORTILLA SOUP BOARD

I love to get a pot of tortilla chicken soup simmering on the stove and invite a few friends over for lunch. Many of the soup ingredients are already stocked in the pantry, and it's easy to keep chicken in the freezer. It all comes together on the board with the soup, your favorite toppings, and good dipping chips. Beautiful and festive, it's perfect for lunch or a light dinner! To save time, make the soup the night before. It's easy to reheat and delicious.

FOR THE BOARD:

24 to 26-inch (60–66 cm) food board

Easy Chicken Tortilla Soup (recipe follows)

1 cup (120 g) grated Mexican cheese

½ red onion, chopped

1 cup (16 g) chopped cilantro

1 cup (240 g) sour cream

1 cup (240 ml) salsa

1 or 2 avocados, peeled, pitted, and sliced

Tortilla chips

FOR THE EASY CHICKEN TORTILLA SOUP:

2 tablespoons (30 ml) olive oil

1 small red onion, chopped

3 cloves garlic, minced

4 cups (960 ml) chicken broth

2 cans (15 ounces, or 420 g) fire-roasted diced tomatoes

2 cans (15 ounces, or 420 g) black beans, rinsed and drained

1 15 ounce can corn, drained

1 tablespoon (6 g) cumin, plus more to taste

½ teaspoon dried oregano

2 whole chicken breasts or 2 to 3 cups (280 to 420 g) chopped rotisserie chicken

2 cups (240 g) shredded cheese (use your favorite)

Salt and pepper

¼ cup (4 g) chopped cilantro

BOARD ASSEMBLY:

1. Place a hot pad in the center of the board for the pot of soup. Arrange the toppings in small bowls on the board. Fill in the open space with tortilla chips.

2. Right before serving, set the pot of soup on the board. Ladle soup into bowls and let each guest add their favorite toppings.

EASY CHICKEN TORTILLA SOUP:

1. In a large pot, heat the oil over medium-low heat. Add the onion and garlic and cook for about 4 minutes, stirring, until soft. Add the remaining soup ingredients to the pot, except for the cheese, salt and pepper, and cilantro. Bring to a boil, then turn down the heat to low and simmer the soup for 1 hour.

2. Remove the chicken breasts from the soup and shred. Put back into the pot. If using rotisserie chicken add it in now. Stir in the shredded cheese. Season with salt and pepper to taste. Garnish with cilantro and serve.

YIELD: 8 or more servings

FAMILY-SIZE NACHO BOARD

Over the years, I've realized it's necessary to have a broad last-minute-meal repertoire. Next to ordering pizza, baked nachos is a go-to on this list. They're easily adaptable to your family's dinner needs. Include different proteins like chicken and beans for a heartier meal, spice it up with fresh jalapeño and salsas, and remember to include pickled chiles or red onion for a bright, acidic touch—oh, and make sure you *don't* skimp on the cheese. Serve with your favorite Mexican desserts, such as churros and Mexican hot chocolate!

FOR THE BOARD:

26-inch (66-cm) food board

2 tablespoons (30 ml) olive oil

3 bell peppers, cored and thinly sliced

16 whole shishito peppers

Kosher salt

1 pound (454 g) blue corn tortilla chips, divided

1 ¾ cups (210 g) shredded sharp Cheddar cheese, divided

1 ¾ cups (210 g) shredded pepper Jack cheese, divided

1 ¾ cups (210 g) shredded mozzarella cheese, divided

1 cup (240 g) black beans, rinsed and drained

1 cup (240 g) white kidney beans, rinsed and drained

1 cup (240 g) red kidney beans, rinsed and drained

1 cup (150 g) corn kernels

1 large chicken breast, cooked and shredded, or 2 cups (280 g) chopped rotisserie chicken

2 jalapeño peppers, thinly sliced

1 cup (240 g) pickled onions (see Tip)

1 cup (150 g) cherry tomatoes, cut in half

2 cups (480 ml) salsa

1 cup (240 g) sour cream

4 limes, cut into wedges

2 cups (480 g) guacamole

BOARD ASSEMBLY:

1. Preheat the oven to 400°F (200°C, or gas mark 6). Line a 12 x 18-inch (30 x 46-cm) baking sheet with parchment paper.

2. On the board, place a trivet or hot pad in the center to hold the baked nachos.

3. In a large frying pan, heat the olive oil until it shimmers. Sauté the bell peppers and shishito peppers for 3 to 4 minutes, until blistered and brown. Add a pinch of salt. Turn them frequently to get a nice, charred look; separate them into 2 bowls and place on the board.

4. Cover a sheet pan with half of the blue tortilla chips. Mix the 3 cheeses together in a large bowl and spread 3 cups (360 g) on top of the chips. In a separate bowl, mix the beans and corn together.

5. Starting in the top left corner of the baking sheet, diagonally spread out the following rows: sautéed bell peppers, mixed beans and corn, shredded chicken with jalapeños, and shishito peppers. Sprinkling the remaining 2 ¼ cups (270 g) cheese on top. Place a piece of parchment paper on top of the nachos, followed by a large piece of foil, to cover the entire baking sheet. Place in the oven and bake for 18 to 20 minutes.

6. Meanwhile, fill bowls with the pickled onions, tomatoes, salsa, sour cream, lime wedges, guacamole, olives, cabbage, and chiles and set around the outer edge of the board.

(CONTINUED)

1 cup (100 g) olives

½ cup (40 g) thinly sliced red cabbage

2 tablespoons (20 g) chopped fire-roasted green chiles

½ cup (8 g) chopped cilantro

8 ounces (224 g) yellow corn tortilla chips

7. When the nachos are done, turn the oven to broil. Remove the foil and parchment paper; broil the nachos for 2 more minutes. Garnish with the cilantro. Set the baking sheet on the board and fill in open areas with the remaining blue tortilla chips and the yellow tortilla chips.

YIELD: 8 or more servings

TIP: For the pickled onions: Thinly slice a small red onion, place in a bowl, and pour over 1 cup (240 ml) white vinegar. Stir to combine.

CHEESY SLOPPY JOE SLIDERS BOARD

To solve the problem of a flimsy, soggy Sloppy Joe, I sought out a binding ingredient, and the solution was clear: add copious amounts of cheese. For this Sloppy Joe board, make the meat the night before so on the day of feasting you can quickly assemble the sliders, pop them in the oven, and set up your board. Another quick tip is to buy your favorite coleslaw and layer it on your sandwich to add a cool crunchy bite to your meaty, cheesy, slider. Don't forget the pickles!

FOR THE BOARD:

20-inch (51-cm) food board

Cheesy Sloppy Joes Sliders (recipe follows)

2 cups (240 g) coleslaw

1 cup (120 g) bacon pieces

¾ cup (180 g) sour cream

1 cantaloupe, sliced

½ small watermelon, sliced

1 pound (454 g) dill pickle spears

2 cups (200 g) corn chips

BOARD ASSEMBLY:

1. Place a hot pad in the center of the board to hold the pan of sliders.

2. Divide the coleslaw between 2 small bowls and place across from each other on the outside of the board. Fill 2 more small bowls with the bacon and sour cream and place across from each other on the outside of the board. On opposite sides of where the sliders will be placed, fan the cantaloupe and watermelon.

3. Set the sliders in the middle of the board. Around it, place the dill pickle spears and fill in any open area with corn chips. Serve hot!

(CONTINUED)

FOR THE CHEESY SLOPPY JOE SLIDERS:

1 tablespoon (15 g) Dijon mustard

2 tablespoons (30 ml) Worcestershire sauce

1 tablespoon (15 ml) red wine vinegar

1 teaspoon paprika

½ teaspoon freshly ground pepper

2 tablespoons (30 ml) olive oil

1 pound (454 g) ground beef (85% lean, 15% fat)

1 teaspoon salt, plus a pinch

1 white onion, finely diced

1 red bell pepper, cored and finely diced

4 cloves garlic, crushed

1 can (10.5 ounces, or 294 g) tomato puree or crushed tomatoes

2 tablespoons (25 g) brown sugar

12 savory butter rolls

6 slices sharp Cheddar cheese

1 tablespoon (15 g) unsalted butter, melted

1 cup (120 g) shredded sharp Cheddar cheese

CHEESY SLOPPY JOE SLIDERS:

1. Preheat the oven to 350°F (180°C, or gas mark 4). Lightly grease the bottom and sides of an 8 x 11-inch (20 x 28-cm) baking dish.

2. In a small mixing bowl, whisk the mustard, Worcestershire, vinegar, paprika, and pepper. Set aside.

3. Heat the olive oil in a large skillet over medium-high heat. Add the ground beef in large chunks and brown for 4 to 5 minutes. When the underside of the meat is golden, break the meat into smaller pieces, then add the mustard mixture and the salt. Stir to combine and continue cooking for 3 to 4 more minutes, until the meat is nearly cooked through. Remove from the pan and set aside.

4. Drain off half the fat, add the onion, bell pepper, garlic, and a pinch of salt. Cook over medium heat until the vegetables have softened, 5 to 7 minutes. Add the meat back to the pan along with the tomato puree and brown sugar. Stir and reduce the heat to medium-low. Cook for 10 minutes, then remove from the heat and set aside.

5. Open the rolls and place face up on a baking sheet. Broil until lightly golden, 1 to 2 minutes. Place the roll bottoms in the prepared baking dish and spread the meat in a single layer; top with the cheese slices, followed by the bun tops.

6. Brush the top of the buns with the melted butter and sprinkle with the shredded cheese. Place a sheet of parchment paper over the cheese and completely cover the pan with foil.

7. Bake for 15 minutes; remove the foil and bake for an additional 10 minutes to allow the shredded cheese to brown (or place under the broiler for a minute or 2).

YIELD: 6 or more servings

GRILLED CHEESE WITH ORANGE BASIL TOMATO SOUP BOARD

This is tomato soup and grilled cheese 2.0. The addition of basil and orange brighten the tomato soup, while the fig jam, prosciutto, pesto, and sun-dried tomatoes elevate your grilled cheese to a level that makes you never want to eat plain grilled cheese again. This soup is also delicious to eat cold, which is a testament to how flavorful it is! Save time and bake the grilled cheese sandwiches all at once. This ensures evenly toasted and cheesy sandwiches that you can serve to everyone at the same time.

FOR THE BOARD:

20-inch (51-cm) food board

Orange Tomato Basil Soup (recipe follows)

4 Sharp Cheddar Fig Prosciutto Grilled Cheese Sandwiches (see Tip)

4 Provolone Pesto Sun-Dried Tomato Grilled Cheese Sandwiches (see Tip)

2 cups (200 g) croutons

4 to 6 slices bacon, cooked and crumbled

½ cup (120 g) crème fraîche

1 Granny Smith

1 Opal apple

1 Honeycrisp apple

Fresh basil, for garnish

BOARD ASSEMBLY:

1. In the center of a board, place a hot pad for the soup. While the soup is cooking, start assembling the grilled cheese sandwiches.

2. Separate the croutons into 2 small bowls and place on the outside edge of the board across from each other. Add 2 small bowls of chopped bacon and crème fraîche across from each other.

3. Fan the apple slices on either side of the board, in between the bowls. When the grilled cheese comes out of the oven, slice in half diagonally and place it with tips up on the board. Place the soup on the hot pad (leave the lid on until ready to serve), then garnish with the basil.

FOR THE ORANGE BASIL TOMATO SOUP:

¼ cup (60 g) unsalted butter

1 medium yellow onion, diced

4 cloves garlic, crushed

2 medium carrots, diced

2 teaspoons (10 g) kosher salt, plus a pinch

¼ cup (60 g) tomato paste

2½ cups (600 ml) vegetable stock

2 teaspoons (4 g) orange zest

¼ cup (60 ml) fresh orange juice

1 can (28 ounces, or 785 g) whole peeled whole tomatoes in juice

1 packed cup (30 g) roughly chopped basil, thick stems removed

2 teaspoons (8 g) freshly ground black pepper, plus more to taste

⅓ cup (80 ml) heavy cream

ORANGE BASIL TOMATO SOUP:

1. Melt the butter in a large saucepan over medium-low heat. Add the onion, garlic, carrots, and a generous pinch of salt. Cook for 12 to 15 minutes, or until the onions are translucent and the carrots are softened.

2. Add the tomato paste and cook for 6 minutes, allowing it to lightly caramelize; stir occasionally. Add the vegetable stock, orange juice and zest, tomatoes, basil, remaining 2 teaspoons salt, and the pepper.

3. Bring to a boil, then reduce the heat and simmer for 30 minutes, stirring every 10 minutes or so. When the soup has thickened slightly, transfer to a blender and puree. You can also use an immersion blender. When the soup is smooth, add the heavy cream and continue blending until silky. Taste for additional salt and pepper.

YIELD: 8 servings

TIP: For the Sharp Cheddar Fig Prosciutto Grilled Cheese Sandwiches: Preheat the oven to 400°F (200°C, or gas mark 6). Butter the outside of 8 slices of white bread and spread 1 tablespoon (15 g) fig jam on the inside of 1 slice. Layer 2 thick slices of sharp Cheddar cheese and prosciutto and close the sandwiches. Place on a baking sheet and bake for 5 minutes per side.

TIP: For the Provolone Pesto Sun-Dried Tomato Grilled Cheese Sandwiches: Preheat the oven to 400°F (200°C, or gas mark 6). Butter the outside of 8 slices of white bread and spread 1 tablespoon (15 g) pesto on the inside of 1 slice. Layer 2 thick slices of sharp provolone cheese and top with 1 tablespoon (10 g) chopped sun-dried tomatoes. Close the sandwiches. Place on a baking sheet and bake for 5 minutes per side.

SUMMER BURGER BOARD

Summer would be incomplete without the aroma of a smoking grill. This Summer Burger Board is laced with subtle smoky flavors that pair perfectly with sweet corn, savory bacon, sharp Cheddar, refreshing lettuce, tangy pickles, and more. Enjoy these burgers for lunch or dinner under the summer sun.

FOR THE BOARD:

26-inch (66-cm) food board

2 pounds (908 g) ground beef

Kosher salt and cracked black pepper

Cooking spray

8 corn cobs, boiled for 4 minutes

8 teaspoons (40 g) mayonnaise

2 tablespoons (2 g) finely chopped cilantro

½ cup (100 g) bread and butter pickles

¼ cup (60 g) pepper bacon jam

¼ cup (60 ml) yellow mustard

⅓ cup (80 g) chipotle aioli

⅓ cup (80 g) ketchup

8 slices Cheddar cheese

8 strips cooked bacon, cut in half

½ honeydew melon, sliced

2 cups (300 g) blackberries

2 cups (300 g) blueberries

1 head iceberg lettuce, cut into wedges

4 Roma tomatoes, sliced

½ red onion, thinly sliced

1 pound (454 g) strawberries

8 pretzel buns, toasted or grilled

BOARD ASSEMBLY:

1. On the board, place a hot pad or trivet where the corn and burgers will be served. Set a plate for the pretzel rolls on the board.

2. To make the burgers, divide the ground beef into 8 patties and place on a cutting board. Sprinkle with kosher salt and pepper; spray both sides with cooking spray. Heat a large skillet over medium-high heat and add the patties. Cook for 2 to 3 minutes for medium-rare, or flip and cook an additional 3 to 4 minutes for medium-done. When cooked, remove from the pan and set aside.

3. After boiling the corn, allow to cool for a couple of minutes. Rub down each cob with 1 teaspoon (5 g) of mayonnaise and season with salt and pepper. Grill or broil, turning occasionally until all sides are browned (2 to 3 minutes on the grill, 3 to 4 minutes broiled). Place on a plate and sprinkle with the cilantro.

4. In the middle of the board, place 5 condiment bowls of pickles, pepper bacon jam, mustard, chipotle aioli, and ketchup.

5. Next to where the burgers will go, lay down the cheese, bacon, melon, blackberries, corn, blueberries, lettuce, tomatoes, and onion. Fill in empty spaces with the strawberries.

6. Right before serving, place the warm burgers on the board and the pretzel buns (toasted) on the plate.

YIELD: 8 servings

DELI SPREAD SANDWICH BOARD

We've served this board for many parties, picnics, and summer gatherings because everyone loves to make their own sandwich! Right before serving, slice the rolls in half, spread them with butter, and lightly toast under the broiler, about 1 minute. The warm, toasted bread helps melt the cheese, contrasting wonderfully with the cold deli meats. If desired, swap out the fruit and add your favorite potato, pasta, or macaroni salad.

FOR THE BOARD:

26-inch (66-cm) food board

2 cups (300 g) strawberries

2 cups (300 g) blackberries

2 cups (300 g) blueberries

2 plums, pitted and sliced

½ cantaloupe, sliced

½ honeydew melon, sliced

½ cup (120 g) chipotle aioli

½ cup (120 ml) yellow mustard

½ cup (100 g) bread and butter pickles

1 small red onion, thinly sliced

16 panini rolls

8 ounces (227 g) sliced roast beef

8 ounces (227 g) sliced smoked ham

8 ounces (227 g) sliced turkey breast

8 ounces (227 g) sliced pastrami

8 slices Cheddar cheese

8 slices Havarti cheese

1 head iceberg lettuce, cut into quarters

4 Roma tomatoes, sliced

1 avocado, peeled, pitted, and halved

BOARD ASSEMBLY:

1. Place a large bowl in the center of the board and fill with the strawberries, blackberries, blueberries, and plums. Around the outside, fan the cantaloupe and honeydew melon.

2. Place the aioli, mustard, pickles, and red onion in small bowls on the board. Around the outside of the board, fan 4 groups of 4 panini rolls. Fold the meat slices into quarters, and place in 4 different sections on the board. Fan the cheeses nearby.

3. Place the lettuce and tomatoes in open sections around the outside of the board, opposite from each other. Place the avocado halves on the board. Serve immediately.

YIELD: 8 servings

NORI TEMAKI SUSHI HAND ROLLS BOARD

While I enjoy sushi and poke bowls at any time of the year, I especially like them in summer, when the warm air perfectly contrasts the cold, fresh fish, piquant wasabi, and crisp pickled ginger. Temaki hand rolls are the perfect (uncomplicated) way to enjoy these ingredients—simply wrap nori sheets into a cone and fill with fresh ingredients. How much easier can it get? You can make sushi rice yourself or pick it up from your local market to save time.

FOR THE BOARD:

20-inch (51-cm) food board

11 ounces (310 g) sushi rice

1 ½ cups (360 ml) water

¼ cup (60 ml) rice vinegar

2 ½ tablespoons (30 g) granulated sugar

1 ¼ teaspoons kosher salt

1 cup (30 g) microgreens

½ large English cucumber, julienned

3 carrots, julienned (orange and yellow)

3 tablespoons (45 g) mayonnaise

1 tablespoon (15 ml) sriracha

1 teaspoon sesame oil

1 pound (454 g) sushi-grade salmon, cut into ½- to ¾-inch (1.3- to 2-cm) cubes

1 teaspoon furikake, for garnish

¼ cup (20 g) sliced scallion

1 pound (454 g) sushi-grade ahi tuna, cut into ½- to ¾-inch (1.3- to 2-cm) cubes

¼ cup (30 g) orange tobiko caviar

¼ cup (30 g) black tobiko caviar

¼ cup (30 g) pickled sushi ginger

1 tablespoon (10 g) wasabi

1 avocado, peeled, pitted, and cut into thin wedges

6 ounces (168 g) shrimp nigiri sushi

10 nori seaweed sheets, cut in half

BOARD ASSEMBLY:

1. In a fine-mesh sieve, or in a large bowl, rinse the rice under cold water, using your hand to gently agitate the grains. Continue rinsing until the water runs mostly clear. Transfer the rice to a large pot and add the water. Soak the rice for at least 30 minutes before cooking. Cover the pot and bring the water to a boil, then lower the heat to a simmer and cook for about 15 minutes. Remove from the heat and steam for another 10 minutes with the lid on. As the rice cooks, make the seasoning; in a small bowl, combine the vinegar, sugar, and salt. Whisk until dissolved, then set aside.

2. When the rice is done steaming, immediately transfer to a large shallow bowl or a large rimmed baking sheet. Use a wooden spoon to gently spread the grains into a single layer—this will allow the rice to cool quickly. Evenly pour the vinegar seasoning over the grains. Use the wooden spoon to gently incorporate the seasoning, being careful not to mash the rice together. The rice is done when fluffy and the temperature is barely warm.

3. Transfer the rice to a bowl and cover with a damp towel. When ready to serve, spray a bowl with nonstick spray; gently pack the rice into the bowl. Flip the bowl over onto a medium plate; tap the top of the bowl, then gently remove the bowl. This will create a perfect bowl shape of rice. Place on the left side of the board. Surround it with the microgreens and cucumber. Lay down the julienned carrots.

6 strawberry ice cream mochi

6 mango ice cream mochi

1 pack (1.4 ounces, or 40 g) strawberry Pocky

1 pack (1.4 ounces, or 40 g) chocolate Pocky

4. In a medium bowl, whisk together the mayonnaise, sriracha, and sesame oil until smooth; add the cubed salmon and gently mix. Garnish with the furikake and a few pieces of scallion. In another medium bowl, place the cubed ahi tuna. Set the bowls on the left side of the board, on each side of the rice.

5. Fill 4 small bowls with the orange and black tobiko, pickled ginger, and wasabi. Place on the right side of the board. Fill in the space between the small bowls with the scallion.

6. Down the center of the board, lay slices of avocado and pieces of shrimp next to each other. On the other half of the board, lay down the nori sheets and mochi. Fill in the remaining space with the Pocky sticks.

YIELD: 8 or more servings

TIP: How to assemble a hand roll: Place a rectangular nori sheet shiny side down. Spread ¼ cup (60 g) sushi rice on the left third of the nori. Add fillings at a diagonal, facing the upper left corner of the sheet, then fold the bottom left corner over the fillings; roll into a cone. Use a piece of rice on the bottom right corner to glue the cone together.

TIP: Keep mochi in the freezer until right before serving!

MEDITERRANEAN CHOPPED SALAD BOARD

I'm a big fan of the deconstructed salad. Not only does separating the ingredients make for a beautiful board design, but it also ensures that each guest can customize their salad to their liking. Simply set out plates or cups and your guests can do the rest!

FOR THE BOARD:

20-inch (51-cm) food board

Balsamic Dressing (store-bought or homemade, see Tip)

2 cans (14 ounces, or 392 g) chickpeas, rinsed and drained

Fresh dill, for garnish

4 Persian cucumbers, cut into 1-inch (2.5-cm) chunks

12 ounces (336 g) feta cheese, cut into 1-inch (2.5-cm) chunks

9 pearl tomatoes, 6 quartered, 3 left whole with stem on

1 medium red onion, thinly sliced

1 cup (120 g) sliced pepperoncini

1 cup (100 g) kalamata olives, halved

1 lemon, cut into wedges

1 cup (30 g) chopped parsley

Pita chips (store-bought or homemade, see Tip)

10 dates, chopped

BOARD ASSEMBLY:

1. Place the dressing in a medium-size bowl on the board. Add the chickpeas and toss to coat. Garnish with the dill.

2. Place the cucumbers, feta, quartered tomatoes, red onion, pepperoncini, and olives in vertical rows on the board.

3. Place the lemon wedges and chopped parsley in 2 small bowls on the board. Fill in open areas with the pita chips and chopped dates. Garnish the board with the remaining whole tomatoes.

YIELD: 8 servings

TIP: For the Balsamic Dressing: In a medium-size bowl, combine ½ cup (120 ml) olive oil, ¼ cup (60 ml) balsamic vinegar, 4 teaspoons (20 ml) lemon juice, 4 teaspoons (20 ml) lime juice, 2 tablespoons (30 ml) honey, and salt and pepper to taste. Blend with a whisk.

TIP: For the Homemade Pita Chips: Preheat the oven to 350°F (180°C, or gas mark 4). Cut 8 mini pita pockets into 4 pieces each. place on a baking sheet and drizzle with 2 to 3 tablespoons (30 to 45 ml) olive oil, then sprinkle with za'atar. Bake for 10 minutes.

SHEET-PAN PIZZA BOARD

This sheet-pan pizza takes a bit more time to make than a frozen one, but I assure you it's worth it. Kids can top their portion of the dough with their favorite sauces, cheeses, and toppings to make it their own. Pair the pizza with a fresh salad for a satisfying meal.

FOR THE BOARD:

20-inch (51-cm) food board

1 tablespoon (15 ml) olive oil

1 pound (454 g) premade pizza dough

Flour, for dusting

¼ cup (60 ml) pesto

¼ cup (60 ml) pizza sauce

3 cups (360 g) shredded Mozzarella cheese, divided

1 cup (100 g) shredded Parmesan cheese, divided

½ cup (16 g) sliced basil leaves, divided

1 large heirloom tomato, sliced

2 ounces (56 g) goat cheese, crumbled

Freshly cracked black pepper

4 ounces (112 g) soppressata or any cured meat

½ cup (50 g) sliced black olives

6 cups (180 g) chopped romaine lettuce

1 cup (150 g) cherry tomatoes

½ small red onion, sliced

⅓ cup (80 ml) Caesar dressing

1 lemon, cut into 8 wedges

BOARD ASSEMBLY:

1. Preheat the oven to 475°F (240°C, or gas mark 9). Coat an 11 x 15-inch (28 x 38-cm) sheet pan with the olive oil.

2. Place 3 hot pads in the center of the board where the pizza will go. It will sit up high.

3. Roll out the dough on a floured surface to the size of the pan, then place in the prepared pan.

4. Spread the pesto on half the dough and the pizza sauce on the other. Sprinkle 1 ½ cups (180 g) of the mozzarella and ½ cup (50 g) of the Parmesan evenly over the sauces.

5. Top the pesto side with ¼ cup (8 g) of the basil leaves, sliced tomato, and goat cheese, and sprinkle with black pepper. On the pizza sauce side, lay down the soppressata and black olives.

6. Spread the remaining 1 ½ cups (180 g) mozzarella cheese over the entire pizza. Transfer to the oven and bake for 15 minutes.

7. Arrange the lettuce around the inside edge of the board. Top with the cherry tomatoes, red onion, and remaining ½ cup (50 g) Parmesan cheese. Add a small mini pitcher with the dressing. Place the lemon wedges by the salad.

8. When the pizza is done, remove from the oven and allow it to sit for 5 minutes. Top the pesto side with the remaining ¼ cup (8 g) basil. Slice the pizza and set the pan on the hot pads.

YIELD: 8 servings

ITALIAN TORTELLINI SALAD BOARD

This salad is the perfect last-minute spring or summer luncheon board. With a few simple ingredients, you can put together a decadent spread in no time. I always include crunchy bread, a small dish of olive oil, and balsamic vinegar for dipping.

FOR THE BOARD:

20-inch (51-cm) food board

1 ½ pounds (680 g) five-cheese tortellini

½ cup (120 g) pesto

1 cup (140 g) artichoke hearts, drained

6 ounces (168 g) olive medley
(variety olives)

3 ounces (84 g) sun-dried tomatoes

10 ounces (280 g) burrata cheese

Olive oil

Sea salt and freshly cracked pepper

6 ounces (168 g) prosciutto

1 ½ heirloom tomatoes, cut into 1-inch
(2.5-cm) chunks

½ cup (75 g) blueberries or sliced
strawberries, for garnish

7 basil leaves, for garnish

Balsamic vinegar, for serving

BOARD ASSEMBLY:

1. Cook the tortellini according to package directions, usually about 2 minutes in boiling water. Do not overcook. Drain and place in a large bowl. Add the pesto and gently mix; set aside to continue cooling.

2. On the board, make 4 equal wedges with the tortellini and a wedge with the artichoke hearts.

3. Fill 2 small bowls with the olives and sun-dried tomatoes and place on either side of the board.

4. Place the burrata on the board. With a spoon, mash it open slightly and drizzle with olive oil. Sprinkle with sea salt and cracked black pepper.

5. Arrange the prosciutto in various places on the board. Fill in any open areas with tomato chunks. Sprinkle the salad with the blueberries and basil leaves. Set out small bowls of olive oil and vinegar. Let everyone make their own deconstructed salad.

YIELD: 8 or more servings

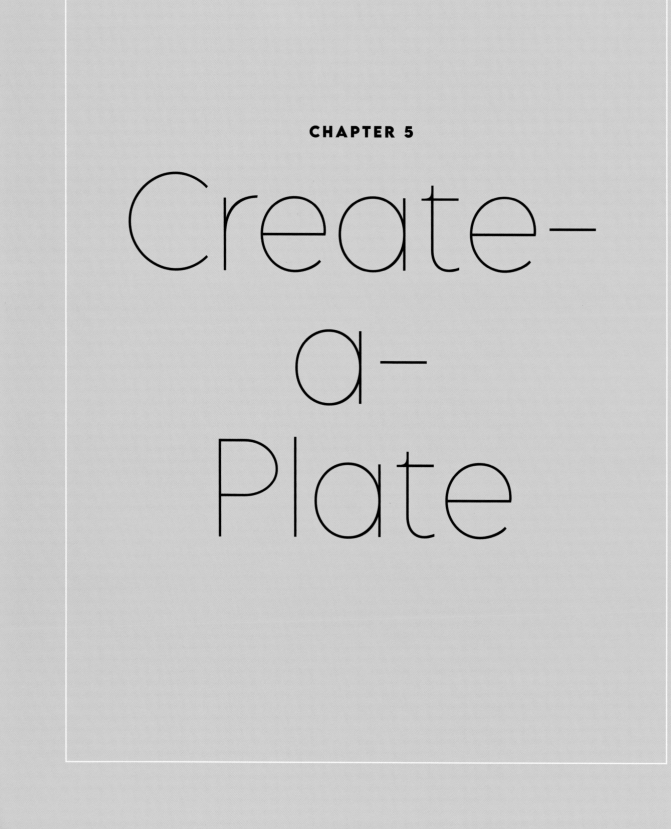

CHAPTER 5

Create-a-Plate

My husband and I love introducing people to each other and fostering friendships and have a reputation for being great "connectors." How? Through something else we love—food! Especially appetizers!

A beautiful appetizer board gives people something GREAT to nibble on and talk about while settling in. And if your appetizer board has the right ingredients, it can even stand in for dinner for both family and friends.

Our favorites encourage family talk, such as the Perfect Party Crostini Board or Mini Brie en Croûte Board. If you're hosting, have guests bring a wedge of crudités, meatballs, wings, and Lit'l Smokies for the Bring-a-Wedge Game Day Board. Or simply set out a Classic Charcuterie Board. It'll be gobbled up within minutes.

But the most delicious part of an appetizer board is the chance to mingle with friends and family!

PERFECT PARTY CROSTINI BOARD

The crostini board is versatile and can be assembled in a matter of minutes. Simply gather toppings like bruschetta, pesto, and tapenade and toast your crostini. You can even take a shortcut and buy premade crostini at your local store. This board is easily adaptable for any season.

FOR THE BOARD:

26-inch (66-cm) food board

2 baguettes (12 ounces, or 336 g), sliced (about 48 crostini), store-bought or homemade (see Tip)

1 jar (7 ounces, or 196 g) roasted pepper bruschetta

1 jar (7 ounces, or 196 g) artichoke bruschetta

1 jar (7 ounces, or 196 g) olive bruschetta

1 jar (7 ounces, or 196 g) olive tapenade

⅓ cup (80 g) pesto

⅓ cup (80 g) sun-dried tomato pesto

¼ cup (60 g) fig jam

2 tablespoons (30 ml) honey

½ cantaloupe, sliced

½ honeydew melon, sliced

2 large heirloom tomatoes (red and yellow), cut into wedges

10 slices fresh mozzarella cheese

8 ounces (227 g) herb Brie wedge

5 ounces (140 g) goat cheese

5 ounces (140 g) prosciutto

5 ounces (140 g) Italian dry salami

2 cups (300 g) blueberries

2 cups (300 g) raspberries

2 cups (300 g) blackberries

Fresh basil sprigs, for garnish

Fresh mint sprigs, for garnish

BOARD ASSEMBLY:

1. Place 2 dinner plates on the board. Leave room in the center for a small bowl. Arrange 24 crostini on each plate.

2. Fill 8 small bowls, fill with the bruschettas, tapenade, pestos, jam, and honey. Place 2 of the bowls in the middle of the dinner plates. Place the other bowls on the board in various places.

3. Fan the sliced cantaloupe and honeydew around each plate. Fan the heirloom tomatoes alternating with mozzarella cheese around the outside of the board.

4. Place the Brie and goat cheese on the board. Arrange the prosciutto and salami around the cheeses, folding the meats into quarters and making flowers.

5. Fill in any gaps with the blueberries, raspberries, and blackberries. Garnish with basil and mint.

YIELD: 16 to 20 servings

TIP: For the crostini: Preheat the oven to 350°F (180°C, or gas mark 4). Peel a few large cloves garlic and rub on each bread slice. Brush with olive oil on both sides. Place on a baking sheet and bake until crisp and lightly golden around the edges, about 15 minutes.

MELT-IN-YOUR-MOUTH CHEESE FONDUE BOARD

To be honest, I don't think I can ever be vegan because I. Love. Cheese. What is more wonderful than dipping your favorite bites into hot, gooey fondue? This fondue board is a cheese lover's dream. If you close your eyes, you just may think you are in the Swiss Alps. To save time, serve with raw veggies instead of roasted.

FOR THE BOARD:

20-inch (51-cm) food board

Cheese Fondue (recipe follows)

1 ½ pounds (680 g) mixed potatoes, cut into 1-inch (2.5-cm) chunks and roasted (page 107)

1 pound (454 g) petite carrots, roasted (page 107)

12 ounces (336 g) summer sausage, cut into 1-inch (2.5-cm) pieces

1 baguette, cut into 1-inch (2.5-cm) slices

1 jar (12 ounces, or 336 g) baby dill kosher pickles, cut into 1-inch (2.5-cm) chunks

1 package (14 ounces, or 392 g) Lit'l Smokies Smoked Sausages, heated

1 can (5.75 ounces, or 160 g) large black olives, drained

8 medium soft pretzels

1 red apple

1 green apple

Lemon juice

10 fondue skewers

FOR THE CHEESE FONDUE:

2 cups (480 ml) dry white wine

1 pound (454 g) Gruyère cheese, grated

1 pound (454 g) aged Cheddar cheese, grated

1 cup (120 g) shredded mozzarella cheese

¼ cup (30 g) cornstarch

8 ounces (224 g) cream cheese, softened

BOARD ASSEMBLY:

1. On the board, place a hot pad for the cheese fondue.

2. Arrange all the items around the hot pad as desired.

3. Core and slice the apples and toss with lemon juice to prevent browning. Fan out on the board.

4. When the fondue is ready, set it on the board and serve with the fondue skewers.

CHEESE FONDUE:

1. In a medium pot, add the wine and bring to a simmer over medium heat. Meanwhile, combine the cheeses in a large bowl and toss with cornstarch.

2. Add cream cheese to the simmering wine and whisk until smooth and melted. Add about ½ cup (60 g) at a time of the cheese mixture, stirring until the cheese melts before adding more. Repeat until all the cheese is added.

3. Decrease the heat to medium-low and cook, stirring constantly, until the cheese is completely melted, about 10 minutes.

4. Stir in the whiskey and lemon juice. Cook, stirring often, until the mixture is bubbling, 1 to 2 minutes. Add the salt, pepper, and nutmeg.

5. Remove from the heat, place a piece of parchment paper over the top of the cheese, then place the lid on top. This prevents the cheese from getting a thick coating on top. Place it on the board and serve immediately.

¼ cup (60 ml) whiskey

2 tablespoons (30 ml) fresh lemon juice

1 teaspoon kosher salt

½ teaspoon black pepper

⅛ teaspoon grated fresh nutmeg (optional)

YIELD: 10 or more servings

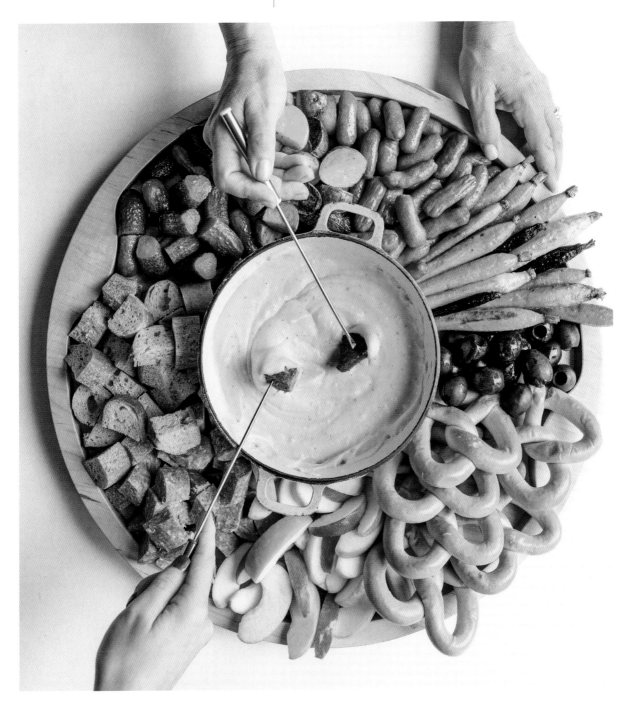

BRING-A-WEDGE GAME DAY BOARD

I know firsthand how expensive it can be to host a party, which is why I came up with the Bring-a-Wedge Game Day Board. You can make the main dish of Beef and Lamb Meatballs, while all of your guests bring their favorite game day appetizer to contribute to a "wedge" on the board. Once your guests arrive, having them assemble the board can be a fun team activity to kick off the night.

FOR THE BOARD:

26-inch (66-cm) food board

Sun-Dried Tomato Hummus (page 58)

Roasted Onion Dip (recipe follows)

1 ½ cups (360 g) marinara sauce

1 ½ cups cranberry jalapeño dip, or other dip

Beef and Lamb Meatballs (recipe follows)

1 package (12 ounces, or 360 g) Beef Lit'l Smokies rolled with 1 package (8 ounces, or 224 g) crescent rolls (see Tip)

24 breaded mozzarella sticks

24 chicken wings

4 large carrots, cut into sticks

15 baby bell peppers

2 Persian cucumbers, sliced lengthwise

6 radishes, halved

2 celery stalks, cut into sticks

8 ounces (227 g) M&M's

¼ cup (60 ml) ketchup

¼ cup (60 ml) mustard

10 to 12 large picks (or small kebabs) for the meatballs

FOR THE ROASTED ONION DIP:

2 medium yellow onions, cut into 8 wedges

2 tablespoons (30 ml) olive oil

1 teaspoon kosher salt, plus more to taste

1 teaspoon freshly ground pepper, plus more to taste

¾ cup (180 g) mayonnaise

BOARD ASSEMBLY:

1. Fill 4 bowls with the hummus, onion dip, marinara sauce, and cranberry jalapeño dip and place evenly spread out along the outside edge of the board.

2. Create 4 wedges on the board between the dips with the meatballs, sausage rolls, mozzarella sticks, and wings. In the open spaces, fill with the carrots, peppers, cucumber, radish, celery, and M&M's. Next to the sausages, place 2 small bowls of ketchup and mustard. Add the picks next to the meatballs for easy dipping.

ROASTED ONION DIP:

1. Preheat the oven to 425°F (220°C, or gas mark 7). Line a baking sheet with foil.

2. Separate the onion layers, place in a large bowl, and toss with the olive oil, salt, and pepper. Place on the center rack of the oven and roast until soft and caramelized, 40 to 45 minutes, tossing the onions midway through.

3. In a food processor, combine the mayonnaise, cream cheese, crème fraîche, lemon juice, vinegar, Worcestershire, roasted onions, and salt and pepper to taste. Blend until combined, then transfer to a mixing bowl and stir in the bacon. Cover the bowl and refrigerate for at least 4 hours before serving to allow the dip to set.

½ cup (120 g) cream cheese, softened

½ cup (120 g) crème fraîche or sour cream

1 ½ teaspoons fresh lemon juice

1 tablespoon (15 ml) sherry vinegar

¾ teaspoon Worcestershire sauce

3 strips thick-cut bacon, cooked and finely chopped (optional)

FOR THE BEEF AND LAMB MEATBALLS:

2 tablespoons (30 g) unsalted butter

1 yellow onion, finely minced

5 cloves garlic, finely minced

2 teaspoons (10 g) salt, plus more to taste

1 pound (454 g) ground beef (80% lean, 20% fat)

1 pound (454 g) ground lamb

½ cup (15 g) finely chopped fresh parsley

¼ cup (4 g) finely chopped fresh chives

1 ½ teaspoons freshly ground pepper

⅓ cup (35 g) panko breadcrumbs

2 eggs, whisked

BEEF AND LAMB MEATBALLS:

1. Preheat the oven to 425°F (220°C, or gas mark 7). Line a large baking sheet with foil.

2. Melt the butter in a large skillet over medium heat. Add the onion and garlic and sauté until translucent, 5 to 6 minutes. Season with salt to taste. Allow to cool and set aside.

3. In a large bowl, combine the beef, lamb, herbs, breadcrumbs, eggs, and onion mixture. Mix well using your hands. If you need to, spray your hands with cooking oil first to prevent the meat from sticking.

4. Divide the meat into thirty 1 ½-inch (4-cm) meatballs, and place on the prepared baking sheet. Place on the center rack and bake for 18 to 20 minutes, until cooked through.

YIELD: 20 or more servings

TIP: For the Beef Lit'l Smokies: Preheat the oven to 375°F (190°C, or gas mark 5). Unroll the can of the dough and separate into 8 triangles. Cut each triangle lengthwise into 4 narrow triangles. Place a sausage on the shortest side of each triangle. Roll up each one, starting at the shortest side of the triangle and rolling to the opposite point. Place the point side down on 2 ungreased cookie sheets. Bake for 12 to 15 minutes, or until golden brown. Serve warm.

HUMMUS AND ROASTED CRUDITÉS BOARD

A crudités platter is one of my favorite ways to use seasonal vegetables. In the fall and wintertime, I choose to roast some of my veggies because it intensifies their flavor and adds warmth. Additionally, I like making homemade hummus, as it adds a personal touch to my board. My guests always enjoy this wholesome, vibrant, flavorful board.

FOR THE BOARD:

26-inch (66-cm) food board

Sun-Dried Tomato Hummus (store-bought or homemade, page 58)

½ cup (120 g) plus 1 teaspoon (5 g) kosher salt, divided

1 pound (454 g) asparagus, trimmed

1 pound (454 g) haricots verts or green beans, trimmed

12 petite carrots

1 pound (454 g) cauliflower florets

1 ½ pounds (680 g) mixed baby potatoes, halved

1 medium red beet, peeled and cut into ¾-1-inch cubes

¼ cup (60 ml) olive oil, divided

¼ cup (4 g) finely chopped cilantro

4 cloves roasted garlic

10 large white button mushrooms

20 baby bell peppers

4 to 5 Persian cucumbers, sliced lengthwise

6 large radishes, halved

2 cups (140 g) broccoli florets

1 pint (300 g) cherry tomatoes

BOARD ASSEMBLY:

1. Place a large bowl in the center of the board to hold the hummus. Make the hummus ahead and refrigerate (for better flavor).

2. Prepare a large bowl of water and ice. Set aside. Bring 6 cups (1440 ml) water to a boil in a large pot and add ½ cup (120 g) of the kosher salt. When the bubbles are vigorous, add the asparagus and haricots verts. When the water returns to a boil, cook for 3 to 4 minutes. Drain the vegetables, then immediately submerge in the ice bath. When the veggies have cooled, remove from the ice water and refrigerate until ready to use.

3. Preheat the oven to 400°F (200°C, or gas mark 6) and line 2 large baking sheets with foil. Spread the carrots and cauliflower on one baking sheet and the potatoes and beet on the other, keeping them well spaced out. Drizzle each pan with 1 tablespoon (15 ml) of the olive oil and the remaining ½ teaspoon (3 g) kosher salt; toss to coat. Place on the center rack of the oven and roast for 15 minutes, then gently toss and roast for 15 to 20 minutes. Let cool.

4. Place the hummus in a large bowl in the center of the board. Drizzle with the remaining 2 tablespoons (30 ml) olive oil and slightly mix in, but not all the way. Top with the cilantro and roasted garlic.

5. Arrange the remaining ingredients around the bowl as desired.

YIELD: 12 or more servings

MINI BRIE EN CROÛTE BOARD

Don't be fooled by the size of these Brie bites—their flavor is mighty. They're easy to prepare and keep in the fridge until you're ready to bake. Prepare the board ingredients beforehand to ensure that you can serve the bites fresh out of the oven. Additionally, make sure the cheese is cold and firm before baking, which will prevent it from leaking out of the puff pastry. Enjoy your bites with a smear of sweet jam, a slice of savory cured meat, or served on a dessert board dipped into chocolate.

FOR THE BOARD:

20-inch (51-cm) food board

Mini Puff Pastry Baked Brie (recipe follows)

¼ cup (60 g) tangerine jam

¼ cup (60 g) strawberry jam

¼ cup (60 g) blueberry jam

3 ounces (84 g) Italian dry salami

3 ounces (84 g) dry coppa

2 whole pomegranates, split

2 blood oranges, sliced

½ cup (75 g) pecans

1 cup (130 g) whole almonds

2 ounces (56 g) cracked pepper crisps

2 ounces (56 g) Raincoast cranberry hazelnut crisps

1 cup (150 g) red grapes

1 cup (150 g) blackberries

Rosemary, for garnish

FOR THE MINI PUFF PASTRY BAKED BRIE:

Flour, for dusting

1 sheet puff pastry, thawed

16 mini Brie wheels or one 12-ounce (340-g) Brie round divided into sixteen 1-inch (2.5-cm) pieces, cold

1 egg whisked with 1 tablespoon (15 ml) water

BOARD ASSEMBLY:

1. Place a plate in the center of the board that will hold the baked Brie bites. Prepare the Brie bites and bake.

2. Fill 3 small bowls with the jams. Set down on the board in a triangle, close to the edge.

3. Fold the meats into quarters to make flowers and arrange around 2 bowls of the jams.

4. Place the pomegranates on opposite sides of the board. Fill in the remaining spaces with the fruit and nuts.

5. When the Brie is done baking, immediately place on the plate and garnish the board with the rosemary.

MINI PUFF PASTRY BAKED BRIE:

1. Preheat the oven to 400°F (200°C, or gas mark 6) and line a baking sheet with parchment paper.

2. On a floured surface, roll out the puff pastry into 12 x 12-inch (30 x 30-cm) square. Cut the pastry into sixteen 3-inch (7.5-cm) squares and place a cold piece of Brie in the center. Tightly and gently stretch the dough around the Brie, bringing the four corners together and pinching the seams to seal the dough. Twist the dough together at the top. Repeat for all 16 squares.

3. Place on the prepared baking sheet, evenly spaced out, and brush with the egg wash. Bake for about 20 to 25 minutes, or until the pastries are golden brown.

YIELD: 8 servings

CLASSIC CHARCUTERIE BOARD

Food is love, but the actual act of serving and making others feel warm and welcome, wherever you are, is what I love. A charcuterie board is a great place to begin. This board is how I got started with the big board concept when 12 of my friends visited for a girl's retreat. There's always a bite for everyone, and it's fun to watch people come up with their own combination. There are no hard rules for making a charcuterie. Make it your own, change it up, think outside the box! (Or, in this case, outside the circle!)

FOR THE BOARD:

26-inch (66-cm) food board

5 ounces (140 g) Gorgonzola cheese

8 ounces (224 g) Gouda cheese

8 ounces (224 g) Fougerus cheese

3 ounces (84 g) herbed goat cheese

8 ounces (224 g) fromage blanc

7 ounces (196 g) pitted olives

7 ounces (196 g) feta Greek salad

¼ cup (60 g) fig jam

¼ cup (60 g) apricot jam

¼ cup (60 g) blackberry jam

1 pomegranate, cut open

7 ounces (196 g) Cabaret butter crackers

5 ounces (140 g) Raincoast cranberry hazelnut crisps

3 ounces (84 g) Raincoast cheese crisps

4 ounces (112 g) sweet coppa

4 ounces (112 g) sweet soppressata

3 ounces (84 g) salami mozzarella sticks

4 ounces (112 g) Italian herb sweet sausage, thinly sliced

3 persimmons, 1 whole for garnish, 1 sliced, 1 wedged

1 blood orange, cut into wedges

1 Honeycrisp apple, cored and sliced

BOARD ASSEMBLY:

1. On a plate in the center of the board, place the 5 cheeses, leaving about 1 inch (2.5 cm) between for slicing.

2. Fill 5 small bowls with the olives, Greek salad, and jams. Place evenly on the board.

3. Slice and cut the pomegranate into quadrants and lay out on the board.

4. Fan out the butter crackers in a snake shape down the middle of the board. Place the crackers on either side of the board, one type fanned out, the other type arranged around one of the jams.

5. Fold the coppa into quarters to make flowers and place around one of the jams. Lay the soppressata next to the cheese plate. Lay down the salami cheese sticks on the inside edge of the board, and opposite of this, fan out the sausage slices.

6. For a garnish, fan out persimmon slices between the mozzarella slices and meat, and lay down persimmon wedges next to one of the olive bowls.

7. Place the sliced orange and apple on the inside edge of the board, fanning them around empty spaces. Fan the plumcot alongside the cheese plate, and the pear at the bottom of the cheese plate. Tuck the blackberries and grapes into empty spaces.

1 plumcot, pitted and sliced

1 red pear, cored and sliced

6 ounces (168 g) blackberries

6 ounces (168 g) red grapes

3 ounces (84 g) Marcona almonds with rosemary

3 ounces (84 g) sweet and spicy pecans

Fresh sage leaves, for garnish

8. Spread the almonds and pecans in any empty spaces and garnish with the sage.

YIELD: 12 or more servings

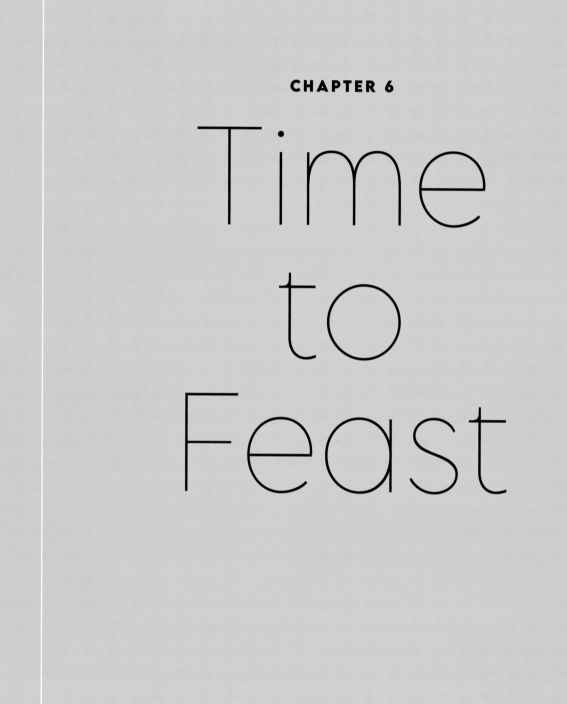

CHAPTER 6

Time to Feast

Nourishing main dish boards are my favorite to make for any occasion: family dinners, potluck gatherings, celebratory events, and more. Never feel like you have to do it all. When guests come for dinner, it's a family affair!

What once was the Taco Bar with toppings spread all over the counter, is now a mobile Taco Board with all the ingredients in one transferable place. The board can be moved from the counter to the center of the table with ease.

In this chapter, you'll find a collection of my favorite, most dependable recipes—the kind you feel comfortable making over and over—like Mac and Cheese, Chili, and Clam Chowder. Some of these recipes will be easily recognizable by my longtime blog readers because they are foolproof dishes that have lived on in my blog for years. I hope you can make them part of your dinner repertoire too!

PISTACHIO LEMON SALMON BOARD

This 30-minute baked salmon recipe comes together beautifully on a dinner board, served with rice and asparagus. Over the years, my eldest son often requested this dish, a true family favorite. Your kids don't eat salmon? They will after you serve this amazing recipe. Want to spruce up your rice? Cook it in broth, and then add dried fruit, nuts, and fresh herbs.

FOR THE BOARD:

24 to 26-inch (60–66 cm) food board

Pistachio Lemon Salmon (recipe follows)

4 cups (800 g) cooked long-grain wild rice

⅓ cup (80 ml) red wine vinaigrette

2 tablespoons (30 g) sea salt

1 ¾ pounds (800 g) asparagus, blanched (see page 107)

1 small watermelon, cut into wedges

6 cups (180 g) mixed greens

8 strawberries, quartered

¼ cup (35 g) fresh blueberries

¼ cup (30 g) sliced cucumber

¼ cup (30 g) crumbled goat cheese

20-ounce (560-g) rustic loaf of bread

¼ cup (60 g) unsalted butter

1 tablespoon (2 g) chopped dill, for garnish

¼ cup (8 g) chopped chives, for garnish

1 lemon, sliced, for garnish

FOR THE PISTACHIO LEMON SALMON:

2-pound (908-g) salmon fillet

1 cup (150 g) pistachio nuts

½ cup (100 g) packed brown sugar

3 tablespoons (45 ml) fresh lemon juice

2 teaspoons (3 g) dill weed

1 ½ teaspoons pepper

BOARD ASSEMBLY:

1. Place a hot pad in the center of the board to hold the large platter of fish and rice.

2. On either side of the platter, place a small bowl with the red wine vinaigrette and a small bowl with the salt (to sprinkle on the watermelon).

3. Place the asparagus and watermelon wedges around the platter. Lay down the mixed greens and top with the berries, cucumber, and goat cheese.

4. Place the bread on a cutting board off to the side with the butter in a small dish.

5. Spread the cooked rice on the large platter and top with the cooked fish. Garnish the salmon with the dill, chives, and lemon slices.

PISTACHIO LEMON SALMON:

1. Preheat the oven to 400°F (200°C, or gas mark 6). Line a baking pan with parchment paper.

2. Rinse the salmon and pat dry with paper towels. Place it on the prepared baking pan.

3. In a small food processor, add half of the pistachio nuts and chop until finely ground. Remove to a small bowl and chop the remaining nuts. Add the brown sugar, lemon juice, dill weed, and pepper and stir to combine. Spread the mixture over the salmon, patting it down to cover the top.

4. Transfer to the oven and bake for 12 to 15 minutes, until the salmon feels firm when pressed with the back of a spatula.

YIELD: 8 servings

ROASTED WHOLE CHICKEN DINNER BOARD

During the colder months, I often use candles to make my home smell warm and inviting. However, I have found that making this balsamic chicken recipe is an equally, if not superior, way to achieve that aroma. It tastes delicious, especially when paired with roasted veggies and a fresh seasonal salad. And a quick tip: Spoon the chicken drippings over the chicken and vegetables before serving.

FOR THE BOARD:

20-inch (51-cm) food board

Balsamic Whole Chicken (recipe follows)

Mixed roasted vegetables (see page 107)

1 head lettuce, cut into wedges

4 tomatoes, sliced

1 cucumber, sliced

¼ cup (60 ml) ranch dressing

1 baguette, sliced

2 tablespoons (30 g) unsalted butter

Chopped parsley, for garnish

FOR THE BALSAMIC WHOLE CHICKEN:

6-pound (2.7-kg) roasting chicken

3 to 4 tablespoons (6 to 8 g) finely chopped fresh thyme

2 to 3 shallots or 1 leek, minced

1 teaspoon salt

1 teaspoon pepper

2 medium red onions, chopped

½ cup (120 ml) dry red wine or reduced-sodium chicken broth

½ cup (120 ml) balsamic vinegar

BOARD ASSEMBLY:

1. Place a hot pad on the board where the chicken and vegetables will be served.

2. Place the lettuce, tomatoes, and cucumbers on the board and place a bowl of ranch dressing nearby.

3. Fan the baguette slices around the inside edge of the board and place a small dish of the butter alongside.

4. Right before serving, place the vegetables on a large plate and set the chicken on top. Sprinkle with chopped parsley for garnish.

BALSAMIC WHOLE CHICKEN:

1. Preheat the oven to 350°F (180°C, or gas mark 4).

2. Wash and pat chicken dry. Remove the giblets.

3. In a small bowl, combine the thyme, shallots, salt, and pepper; rub the mixture under the skin of the chicken.

4. Place the onions in a roasting pan (with a lid); top with the chicken, skin side up. Pour the wine and balsamic vinegar over the chicken. Place the lid back on the dish. Bake, covered, for 1 hour.

5. Remove the lid and bake for another 1 hour, or until a meat thermometer reads 180°F (82°C). The chicken will be nice and brown! Let stand for 15 minutes before carving.

6. Pour the onion sauce into a small bowl and skim off the fat. Place on the board and serve.

YIELD: 4 or more servings

MAKE-YOUR-OWN LASAGNA RAMEKINS BOARD

In my opinion, the Bolognese sauce is the star of this board. While it takes some elbow grease and time to make, the flavors are well worth it. The whole plum tomatoes are a less traditional ingredient, so if you're a Bolognese purist, omit the tomatoes and add 3½ cups (840 ml) more stock. The deconstructed elements allow guests to individualize their serving. To save time, buy canned or premade sauces instead. The Bolognese recipe makes about 6 cups (1440 g), but you only need 4 cups (960 g). Freeze the remaining sauce for another meal.

FOR THE BOARD:

26-inch (66-cm) food board

Eight 14-ounce (392-g) ramekins

4 cups (960 g) Bolognese Sauce (recipe follows)

4 cups (960 g) Spinach Ricotta Filling (see Tip)

2 cups (480 ml) Cheesy Béchamel Sauce (page 27)

1 cup (240 g) pesto

16 sheets oven-ready lasagna noodles

24 slices mozzarella cheese

1 pound (454 g) spring lettuce mix

1 cup (150 g) cherry tomatoes, halved

1 cucumber, sliced

½ red onion, thinly sliced

1 cup (240 ml) Caesar dressing

1 avocado

Parsley, for garnish

BOARD ASSEMBLY:

1. Around the board, arrange the ramekins. Arrange 2 large bowls and 2 medium bowls on the board with 3 hot pads or trivets. These will hold the Bolognese, ricotta filling, béchamel, and pesto.

2. Fan one inside edge with the lasagna noodles. Circle one of the smaller bowls with the mozzarella cheese.

3. Lay down the lettuce, filling the empty spaces around the bowls. Add the tomatoes, cucumbers, and onions on top. Place a small pitcher with the dressing nearby. Slice an avocado and lay down near the salad.

4. When ready to serve, fill the bowls with the sauces. Add parsley in any open areas to garnish.

5. Instruct guests how to make one portion: Break 2 sheets of lasagna noodles into pieces and cover the bottom of a ramekin with some. On top, spread ½ cup (120 g) Bolognese sauce and 1 slice of cheese, then add more noodle pieces. Next, spread ½ cup (120 g) ricotta filling and top with 1 slice of cheese. Add more noodle pieces, 1 slice of cheese, and spread with ¼ cup (60 ml) béchamel to completely cover the noodles. Cover each ramekin with a small piece of parchment paper first, and then foil. Place all the ramekins on a baking sheet and bake at 425°F (220°C, or gas mark 7) for 30 minutes.

FOR THE BOLOGNESE SAUCE:

2 tablespoons (30 ml) olive oil

1 pound (454 g) lean ground beef

1 pound (454 g) lean ground pork

Kosher salt

8 ounces (224 g) pancetta, preferably thick cut, chopped

1 yellow onion, finely minced

3 large celery stalks, finely chopped (about 2 cups, or 240 g)

2 large carrots, finely chopped (about 2 cups, or 240 g)

¾ cup (180 ml) dry white wine

¼ cup (60 g) tomato paste

1 can (28 ounces, or 785 g) whole plum tomatoes, crushed

2 cups (480 ml) chicken stock

Generous pinch of nutmeg, preferably freshly grated

Parmesan cheese rind (optional)

1 fresh bay leaf

⅔ cup (160 ml) heavy cream

½ cup (50 g) grated Parmesan plus

Black pepper

BOLOGNESE SAUCE:

1. Heat a 5-quart Dutch oven over medium-high heat; add the oil. When the oil is hot, add the ground beef and pork. Break the meat into smaller pieces with a wooden spoon, then let sit, undisturbed, for about 4 minutes until the meat has browned. Season with salt and continue cooking until the meat is fully cooked, 7 minutes or so. Transfer the meat to a bowl.

2. Add the pancetta to the rendered fat and reduce the heat to medium-low; cook for 10 minutes. Transfer to the bowl of meat, leaving the rendered fat in the pot.

3. Add the onion, celery, and carrot to the pot and season with a pinch of salt. Cook over medium-low heat for 15 to 20 minutes, until lightly caramelized. Pour in the wine and cook for additional 8 minutes, scraping the bottom of the pan, until the wine cooks off. Add the tomato paste. Stir and allow the paste to caramelize for 5 to 7 minutes.

4. Add the tomatoes, stock, nutmeg, Parmesan rind (if using), and bay leaf. Bring the liquid to a boil, then reduce the heat to low and simmer for 45 minutes to 1 hour, until reduced and thickened.

5. When the Bolognese is done, skim off any excess fat and remove the Parmesan rind and bay leaf. Stir in the heavy cream and Parmesan cheese and season to taste with salt and pepper.

YIELD: 8 servings

TIP: For the Spinach Ricotta Filling: In a large bowl, add 8 ounces (224 g) thawed frozen spinach (excess water squeezed out), 2 cups (480 g) full-fat ricotta cheese, ½ cup (50 g) grated Parmesan, ½ cup (60 g) grated asiago or provolone cheese, 10 large finely chopped basil leaves or 1 tablespoon (4 g) finely chopped parsley or 1 teaspoon Italian seasoning, 1 beaten egg, and ½ teaspoon kosher salt. Stir to combine.

GNOCCHI DINNER BOARD

Pasta nights were staples in our house when my kids were in high school. Regular pasta, however, can often be a bit . . . boring. Gnocchi, the delicious and delicate Italian dumpling, is arguably a tastier vehicle for sauce because it comes in many textures and flavors, fluffy ricotta gnocchi, denser potato gnocchi, and flavorful sweet potato gnocchi. Give this flavorful dumpling board a try for your next pasta night. The Pumpkin Sage Alfredo Sauce and Bolognese can be made in advance.

FOR THE BOARD:

24 to 26-inch (60–66 cm) food board

2 pounds (908 g) gnocchi, prepared according to package directions and kept warm

5 cups (1200 g) Bolognese Sauce (page 123)

1 ½ cups (360 g) Pumpkin Sage Alfredo Sauce (recipe follows)

¾ cup (180 g) basil pesto

3 tablespoons (45 ml) olive oil

1 bunch baby Tuscan kale

2 cups (240 g) sliced squash or zucchini, ½–¾-inch thick

1 bunch asparagus, ends removed

1 loaf French bread, sliced

¼ cup (60 g) unsalted butter

3 heirloom tomatoes, sliced

Fresh parsley, for garnish

FOR THE PUMPKIN SAGE ALFREDO SAUCE:

3 tablespoons (45 g) unsalted butter

3 cloves garlic, pressed

16–8 sage sprigs

1 ¼ cups (300 ml) heavy cream

¼ cup (60 g) pumpkin puree

½ teaspoon kosher salt, plus more to taste

½ teaspoon freshly ground black pepper

⅓ cup (80 ml) reserved pasta water (from cooking the gnocchi)

½ cup (50 g) grated Parmigiano-Reggiano

BOARD ASSEMBLY:

1. Place 4 hot pads on the board to hold the gnocchi, Bolognese, Alfredo sauce, and sautéed vegetables. Fill a small bowl with the pesto and place on the board.

2. Heat the olive oil in a 12-inch (30-cm) skillet over medium-high heat. When oil is shimmery, add the squash, kale, and asparagus and toss in the oil to coat. Allow the squash to sit, undisturbed, for about 2 minutes before stirring. Season the vegetables with salt and pepper to taste. Sauté the squash for an additional 3 to 4 minutes before removing from the heat. Cook the kale until the leaves soften and deepen in color—3 to 5 minutes. Cook the asparagus, stirring semi-frequently until tender with a slight crunch—3 to 8 minutes depending on the size of the stalk. Remove the veggies to a bowl and keep warm. Serve with fresh lemon and parsley.

3. Fan the French bread around the inside edge of half of the board. Set the butter dish next to the bread. Layer the tomatoes between the bowls in the center of the board. Garnish with parsley.

4. Fill the bowls with the gnocchi and sauces.

PUMPKIN SAGE ALFREDO SAUCE:

1. In a large skillet, heat the butter over medium-low heat, then add the garlic and sage. Cook for 3 to 5 minutes, until the garlic has softened, and the sage is fragrant. Using tongs, remove the sage sprigs (shake off excess oil); toss the sprigs.

2. Whisk in the heavy cream, pumpkin puree, salt, and pepper. Bring to a boil, then reduce heat to low and simmer; until sauce thickens, 7 to 10 minutes.

3. Add the reserved pasta water and cook for 2 to 3 minutes. Remove from the heat and stir in the cheese. Place a sheet of wax paper on top of the sauce until ready to serve.

YIELD: 8 servings

THAI-INSPIRED CHICKEN DINNER BOARD

Grilling is essential to summer—my family grills *at least* four times a week during the warmer months. Chicken thighs are often my go-to meat. Not only are they flavorful and fatty, but they're also forgiving if overcooked. Try these Thai-inspired, garlicky chicken thighs for your next summer barbecue. Enjoy alongside grilled veggies, sweet and sour cucumber salad, warm jasmine rice, and vibrant tropical fruits.

FOR THE BOARD:

26-inch (66-cm) food board

Thai-Inspired Garlic Chicken Thighs (recipe follows)

Crushed Cucumber Shallot Salad (recipe follows)

2 cups (330 g) jasmine rice, cooked according to package directions

4 baby zucchinis, quartered lengthwise

3 bell peppers, sliced lengthwise

6 ounces (168 g) green beans

4 ounces (112 g) shishito peppers, whole

2 shallots, cut crosswise into ½-inch (1.3-cm) pieces

2 tablespoons (30 ml) avocado or canola oil

1 ½ teaspoons kosher salt

2 dragon fruits, scooped out (save the shell for garnish)

5 kiwis, peeled and sliced

2 papaya, peeled, seeded, and cubed

2 mangos, peeled, pitted, and cubed

1 pound (454 g) strawberries, halved with stems on

10 ounces (280 g) red sweet chili sauce, divided

1 cup (16 g) cilantro leaves

1 cup (30 g) mint leaves
2 scallions, chopped

2 tablespoons (16 g) chopped peanuts

1 red jalapeño pepper, finely chopped

4 limes, quartered

BOARD ASSEMBLY:

1. Place 4 medium bowls on the board to hold the chicken, cucumber salad, rice, and grilled veggies. Place hot pads under 3 of the bowls (for chicken, rice, and veggies). Prepare a grill for high heat.

2. Place all the veggies in a bowl. Add the oil and salt and toss to coat. Grill on high heat for 6 to 8 minutes or sauté on the stovetop. Do not overcook.

3. Arrange all the fruit on the board, filling the dragon fruit shells for a fun fruit cup.

4. Divide the sweet chili sauce into 2 small bowls and place on the board.

5. Fill 6 bowls with the scallions, cilantro, mint, peanuts, lime wedges, and jalapeño.

6. Transfer the cooked chicken to a bowl on the board. Place bowls of cilantro and mint near the chicken for garnish. Fill another bowl with the rice and place a bowl of the scallion nearby for garnish. Fill another bowl with the cucumber salad, and place bowls with the chopped peanuts and jalapeño nearby for garnish. Fill the last bowl with the grilled veggies, laying them down in a circular fashion.

7. Fill any open areas with remaining herbs and the lime wedges.

(CONTINUED)

FOR THE THAI-INSPIRED GARLIC CHICKEN THIGHS:

1 cup (16 g) cilantro, leaves and stems

½ cup (15 g) basil, preferably Thai basil

2 scallions, chopped, plus 2 tablespoons (10 g) cut diagonally for garnish

⅓ cup (80 ml) soy sauce

⅓ cup (80 ml) fish sauce

2 tablespoons (30 ml) avocado or canola oil, plus more to grill

1 teaspoon ground white pepper

8 to 10 cloves garlic, peeled

2-inch (5-cm) piece ginger, quartered

⅓ cup (65 g) coconut sugar

3 to 4 pounds (1350 to 1800 g) chicken thighs, excess fat removed, rinsed, and patted dry

FOR THE CRUSHED CUCUMBER SHALLOT SALAD:

1 English cucumber

1 large shallot, thinly sliced

1 Thai bird's eye chile, finely chopped

⅓ cup (80 ml) white or rice vinegar

¼ cup (50 g) coconut sugar or granulated sugar

1 heaping teaspoon finely grated ginger

3 tablespoons (45 ml) water

1 teaspoon lime zest

Juice of 1 lime

1 teaspoon toasted sesame oil

1 teaspoon red pepper flakes (optional)

½ teaspoon kosher salt, plus more to taste

½ cup (8 g) whole cilantro leaves, divided

½ cup (15 g) mint leaves, divided

½ cup (65 g) roasted peanuts, roughly chopped, divided

1 tablespoon (8 g) mixed sesame seeds (optional)

THAI INSPIRED GARLIC CHICKEN THIGHS:

1. In a food processor, blend together the cilantro, basil, scallion, soy sauce, fish sauce, oil, white pepper, garlic, ginger, and coconut sugar.

2. Place chicken in a large zip-top bag and pour in the marinade. Press most of the air out, and gently squish the bag to coat the chicken. Allow the thighs to marinate for at least 3 hours, preferably overnight. Grill as desired.

CRUSHED CUCUMBER SHALLOT SALAD:

1. Lay the cucumber on a cutting board and smash it with a heavy object (small heavy pan), to split and crack it. Roughly chop the smashed cucumber into ½-inch (1.3-cm) pieces. Place in a medium-size mixing bowl along with the shallots and chile. Set aside.

2. In a small saucepan over medium heat, combine the rice vinegar, coconut sugar, ginger, and water. Bring to a boil, then reduce to a simmer. Stir until the sugar dissolves and the liquid reduces, 3 to 4 minutes. Stir in the lime zest, lime juice, sesame oil, red pepper flakes, and salt to taste. Pour into a separate container and allow to cool for 10 minutes.

3. When the sauce has cooled, pour it into the bowl with the cucumber. Toss to combine; place in the refrigerator for 2 hours or overnight to chill.

4. When ready to serve, toss the salad with half the cilantro, half the mint leaves, and half the roasted peanuts, and half the sesame seeds, if using. Season with salt, if needed. Garnish with the remaining cilantro, mint, peanuts, and sesame seeds.

YIELD: 8 servings

EPIC BAKED POTATO BOARD

Paul, my husband, is a true Irishman (his parents were Irish immigrants). To him, mayonnaise is a spice, so putting chili and other toppings on a baked potato was a groundbreaking culinary experience for him. I may be exaggerating a bit, but seriously, you can do wonders by adding these toppings to a classic baked potato.

FOR THE BOARD:

26-inch (66-cm) food board

10 large russet potatoes

Extra virgin olive oil

Sea salt and freshly cracked black pepper

4 to 5 cups (960 to 1200 g) Three-Bean Chili (page 140)

2 packages (5 ounces, or 140 g) mixed spring lettuce

½ cup (120 ml) ranch dressing

1 cup (120 g) shredded Cheddar cheese

¼ cup (4 g) chopped cilantro or chives

1 cup (140 g) cooked chopped bacon

1 cup (240 g) sour cream

½ cup (75 g) sliced black olives

¼ cup (40 g) chopped red onion

1 pint (300 g) cherry tomatoes

1 cucumber, sliced

1 cup (150 g) blueberries

16 strawberries

½ cup (120 g) unsalted butter

BOARD ASSEMBLY:

1. Set a hot pad and a large platter in the center of the board to hold the baked potatoes.

2. Preheat the oven to 350°F (180°C, or gas mark 4). Using a fork or small knife, poke small holes all over the skin of each potato. Rub the potatoes with olive oil and a pinch of salt and pepper (this will create crispy skin). Place the potatoes directly on the oven rack (no sheet pan required) and bake for 1 hour or so, until the skin is crispy, and the center is tender.

3. Divide the chili into 2 separate bowls and place one on each side of the board.

4. Arrange the lettuce on opposite sides of the board. Fill a small, spouted container with the ranch dressing.

5. Fill 6 small bowls with the cheese, cilantro, bacon, sour cream, olives, and onion. Set 3 on each side of the board.

6. Place the tomatoes next to the lettuce piles. Fan the cucumber slices around a bowl on either side.

7. Fill open spaces on each side with the blueberries and strawberries.

8. Right before serving, slice the potatoes open and add a pat of butter, then season with salt and pepper. Place on the platter on the board.

YIELD: 10 servings

BEST CLAM CHOWDER BOARD

I love the magic of soup season—the comfort and ease of gathering around the table with family and friends. And clam chowder always brings a little magic to the table! My Best Clam Chowder video went viral on Facebook a few years back because of one controversial ingredient: bacon! Who knew that America's favorite breakfast meat could cause such a debate? Controversy aside, I am still a strong advocate for the addition of bacon, and I think you will be too!

FOR THE BOARD:

26-inch (66-cm) food board

Best Clam Chowder (recipe follows, or use store-bought)

5 cups (150 g) shredded lettuce

2 pounds (908 g) baby shrimp (see Tip)

1 cup (240 ml) cocktail sauce

Parsley, for garnish

2 baguettes, sliced

¼ cup (60 g) unsalted butter

3 cups (150 g) oyster crackers

6 ounces (168 g) Ritz crackers

FOR THE BEST CLAM CHOWDER:

12 slices bacon

¼ cup (60 g) unsalted butter

4 celery stalks, chopped

2 leeks or 1 shallot, finely chopped

2 large onions, chopped

4 to 6 cloves garlic, minced

6 to 8 small red or Yukon Gold potatoes, cubed into ½-inch (1.3-cm) pieces (optional to peel)

3 cups (720 ml) chicken or vegetable broth

1 teaspoon salt

1 teaspoon white pepper

1 teaspoon dried thyme

⅔ cup (80 g) all-purpose flour

4 cups (960 ml) half-and-half, divided

6 cans (6 ½ ounces, or 182 g) chopped clams, drained

BOARD ASSEMBLY:

1. Place a hot pad in the center of the board for the clam chowder.

2. To make the shrimp cocktails, add a ½ cup (15 g) shredded lettuce to 10 small cups. In a medium bowl, add the shrimp and cocktail sauce and gently stir, being careful not to break the shrimp. Add ⅓ cup (80 g) of the shrimp cocktail mixture on top of the lettuce. Add a sprig of parsley to garnish. On the inside edge of the board, on either side, place 5 shrimp cocktails.

3. In between the shrimp cocktails, on the inside edge of the board, fan the baguette slices. Place a small bowl with the butter nearby.

4. In a circular pattern, fan out the Ritz crackers, then add oyster crackers. Garnish any open spaces with the parsley.

BEST CLAM CHOWDER:

1. In a Dutch oven, cook the bacon over medium heat until crisp. Remove to paper towels to drain; set aside. When cool, crumble the bacon.

2. Add the butter to the drippings (you can spoon out some of the drippings if you don't want to use that much) and sauté the celery, leeks, and onions until tender, 5 to 7 minutes. Add the garlic and cook 1 minute longer. Stir in the potatoes, broth, salt, pepper, and thyme. Bring to a boil. Reduce the heat and simmer, uncovered, for 10 to 15 minutes, or until the potatoes are tender.

(CONTINUED)

2 bottles (8 ounces, or 224 g) clam juice

2 to 3 bay leaves

Chopped fresh chives or scallion,
    for garnish

3. In a small bowl, combine the flour and 1 cup (240 ml) of the half-and-half until smooth. Gradually stir into the soup. Bring to a boil; cook and stir for 1 to 2 minutes, or until thickened.

4. Stir in the clams, clam juice, and remaining 3 cups (720 ml) half-and-half; heat through (do not boil). Turn the heat down to low and add the bay leaf. Cook for additional 2 to 3 minutes. Add half of the crumbled bacon.

5. Garnish the chowder with the remaining bacon and chives.

YIELD: 10 servings

TIP: Soak the shrimp in milk or rice vinegar half an hour before making the shrimp cocktail to remove any iodine taste and fishy smell. Rinse and drain before adding the cocktail sauce.

THREE-BEAN CHILI AND CORN BREAD BOARD

Autumn is one of my favorite seasons, as it is the time of transition from cool summer foods to hearty and warm comfort foods. This chili board is perfect for a potluck and game day gathering, or even just a cozy family dinner.

FOR THE BOARD:

24 to 26-inch (60–66 cm) food board

Three-Bean Chili (recipe follows)

1 box (15 ounces, or 420 g) corn bread mix (see Tip)

Grated Mexican cheese blend

Finely chopped cilantro

Finely chopped red onion

Sour cream

Finely chopped scallion

Corn chips

Jalapeño peppers, for garnish

BOARD ASSEMBLY:

1. Place a hot pad in the center of the board where the chili will go. While the chili is cooking, bake the corn bread according to package directions.

2. Around the inside edge of the board, add small bowls filled with the chili condiments. Fill in open areas with squares of corn bread and corn chips. Garnish with jalapeño peppers.

3. Place the chili on the hot pad and keep the lid on until right before serving.

(CONTINUED)

FOR THE THREE-BEAN CHILI:

6 tablespoons (90 ml) olive oil, divided

1 large white onion, diced

3 large (or 5 to 6 small) cloves garlic, pressed

1 ½ teaspoons kosher salt, plus more to taste

Black pepper to taste

2 pounds (908 g) ground turkey

2 teaspoons (4 g) paprika

2 tablespoons (12 g) cumin

1 ½ tablespoons (9 g) chili powder

2 cans (28 ounces, or 785 g) crushed tomatoes

1 can (14 ounces, or 392 g) black beans, rinsed and drained

1 can (14 ounces, or 392 g) red kidney beans, rinsed and drained

1 can (14 ounces, or 392 g) cannellini beans, rinsed and drained

THREE-BEAN CHILI:

1. Heat 3 tablespoons (45 ml) of the olive oil in an 8-quart (7.2-L) stockpot over medium-high heat. Once the oil is shimmering, add the onion and garlic. Lower the heat to medium and stir. Season with salt and pepper to taste and cook until the onions are translucent, 7 to 8 minutes. Transfer the onions and garlic to a small bowl and set aside.

2. In the same pot, heat the remaining 3 tablespoons (45 ml) olive oil over medium-high heat. Once the oil is hot, add the ground turkey, making sure it sizzles when it hits the bottom of the pot. Leave the meat to brown, undisturbed, for 3 to 4 minutes. Using a spatula, gently lift a piece to inspect the color. When the meat is mostly golden on the bottom, begin breaking it into smaller chunks and reduce the heat to medium. Add the 1½ teaspoons salt, paprika, cumin, chili powder, and a few cracks of fresh pepper. Stir to combine and cook for 7 minutes.

3. Stir in the tomatoes, beans, and cooked onion. Bring the chili to a simmer and cook for 1 hour, stirring every 20 minutes.

YIELD: 10 or more servings

TIP: While the corn bread is baking, whip ¼ cup (60 g) unsalted butter with 2 tablespoons (30 g) honey in a small bowl. Remove corn bread from the oven and immediately slather with the whipped butter combo. Allow to sit for a few minutes, then cut into 12 pieces.

OOEY GOOEY MAC AND CHEESE BOARD

I think we can all agree that boxed mac and cheese is delicious, powdered cheese and all. But sometimes, it doesn't quite satisfy our comfort food needs because it's missing a little something, and that something is real cheese. Enter the Ooey Gooey Mac and Cheese Board. This decadently cheesy dish will undoubtedly bring the comfort you've been looking for, and maybe even a post-meal nap, too. This recipe is adapted from my friend Laurel's favorite Martha Stewart Mac and Cheese recipe, and it won't disappoint!

FOR THE BOARD:

26-inch (66-cm) food board

Ooey Gooey Mac and Cheese (recipe follows)

2 jalapeño peppers, sliced

¼ cup (60 g) basil pesto

½ red onion, diced

8 slices bacon, cooked and chopped

½ cup (50 g) sliced scallion

⅓ cup (80 g) fig jam

½ cup (120 ml) balsamic salad dressing

2 Honeycrisp apples, cored and sliced

6 cups (180 g) torn lettuce

½ cucumber, sliced

½ cup (75 g) cherry tomatoes

3 mini orange peppers, sliced

4 ounces (112 g) sweet dry sausage, sliced

4 ounces (112 g) spicy coppa

1 Anjou pear, cored and sliced

1 pound (454 g) red grapes

Fresh basil, for garnish

BOARD ASSEMBLY:

1. On a large board, place a double hot pad or trivet and leave a space for the mac and cheese.

2. Fill 7 small bowls with the jalapeños, pesto, onion, bacon, scallion, fig jam, and balsamic dressing. Arrange on the board.

3. Starting at the top of the board, fan the sliced apples. Add the lettuce to half of the board, topping with the cucumber, tomatoes, and mini peppers.

4. Add the sausage and coppa in flowers around the pesto.

5. Lay the grapes down and fan the sliced pear in any empty space. Set the hot mac and cheese dish on the board and garnish with fresh basil.

FOR THE OOEY GOOEY MAC AND CHEESE:

1 ⅓ cups (105 g) panko breadcrumbs

½ teaspoon garlic powder

½ teaspoon paprika

8 tablespoons (120 g) unsalted butter, divided

2 teaspoons (10 g) salt, plus more for the breadcrumbs, divided

¼ teaspoon freshly grated pepper, plus more for the breadcrumbs, divided

4 ½ cups (1080 ml) whole milk

½ cup (60 g) all-purpose flour

½ teaspoon ground nutmeg

4 cups (about 18 ounces, or 500 g) grated sharp white Cheddar cheese, divided

2 cups (about 8 ounces, or 230 g) grated regular Cheddar cheese, divided

1 ½ cups (180 g) grated mozzarella cheese, divided

1 pound (454 g) elbow macaroni

OOEY GOOEY MAC AND CHEESE:

1. Preheat the oven to 375°F (190°C, or gas mark 5). Butter a 3½-quart (3-L) casserole dish and set aside.

2. Combine the breadcrumbs, garlic powder, paprika, and 2 tablespoons (30 g) of the butter in a skillet and cook over medium heat, stirring constantly, until browned, 2 minutes. Season with salt and pepper to taste.

3. In a medium pan, heat the milk over medium heat.

4. Melt the remaining 6 tablespoons (90 g) butter in a large skillet over medium heat. When the butter bubbles, add the flour and cook, stirring constantly, for 1 minute. Pour the hot milk into the flour mixture, whisking while pouring, until the mixture bubbles and becomes thick.

5. In a small bowl, mix together ½ cup (60 g) of the sharp Cheddar, ½ cup (60 g) of the regular Cheddar, and ½ cup (60 g) of the mozzarella cheeses. Set aside

6. Remove the pan from the heat and stir in the remaining 2 teaspoons (10 g) salt, remaining ¼ teaspoon pepper, nutmeg, remaining 3 ½ cups (440 g) sharp Cheddar, remaining 1 ½ cups (210 g) regular Cheddar cheese, and ½ cup (60 g) of the mozzarella cheese. Stir until the cheese melts, then set cheese sauce aside.

7. Fill a large saucepan with water and bring to a boil. Add the macaroni and cook for 2 minutes *less* than the package directions. Transfer the macaroni to a colander, rinse under cold running water, and drain well. Stir the macaroni into the cheese sauce.

8. Pour half the mixture into the prepared casserole dish. Sprinkle with the remaining ½ cup (60 g) mozzarella cheese. Pour the remaining mixture into the casserole dish. Top with the reserved mixed cheeses. Bake for 20 minutes. Remove from the oven and sprinkle with the breadcrumbs. Bake for an additional 10 minutes. Cool for 5 minutes before serving.

YIELD: 12 or more servings

FESTIVE TACO DINNER BOARD

Taco Tuesday is one of my family's favorite nights of the week. Our style of tacos often features rice, beans, and taco meat, topped with a generous helping of cheese. Serve this board with your favorite sides, and don't forget the hot sauce! Finish off the meal with fried ice cream and churros.

FOR THE BOARD:

26-inch (66-cm) food board

30 crunchy corn taco shells

3 recipes Basic Taco Meat (page 55)

2 cups (240 g) shredded Mexican cheese

1 cup (16 g) chopped cilantro, divided

1 cup (240 g) sour cream

½ small red onion, chopped

4 ounces (112 g) sliced black olives

10 ounces (280 g) guacamole

1 cup (240 g) corn salsa

10 ounces (280 g) fresh salsa

8 ounces (224 g) tricolored corn tortilla chips

12 ounces (336 g) shredded lettuce

2 cups (300 g) chopped tomatoes

4 to 5 limes, sliced

3 habanero peppers, for garnish

taco sauce, for serving

BOARD ASSEMBLY:

1. Preheat the oven to 350°F (180°C, or gas mark 4).

2. Fill the taco shells with the meat and cheese. Place on a baking sheet and bake for 5 minutes. Remove from the oven and top with ½ cup (8 g) of the cilantro.

3. Arrange tacos on the outside of the board in 4 sections.

4. Fill small bowls with the sour cream, red onion, black olives, guacamole (sprinkled with a few pieces of cilantro), corn salsa, fresh salsa, and remaining ½ cup (8 g) cilantro. Use the bowls to separate the rows of tacos. This will hold the tacos in place. Set the guacamole in the center of the board.

5. In an empty space in the center of the board, lay down the corn chips. Arrange the lettuce around a bowl. Surround a bowl with the chopped tomatoes.

6. Place the lime slices in any open areas on the board and garnish with the habanero peppers. Serve with your favorite taco sauce.

YIELD: 10 or more servings

WHOLESOME BOWLS BOARD

This board was made with leftovers in mind. Often, I find I have random tubs of leftovers, like roasted veggies, soft-boiled eggs, meats, and grains. While you can use all fresh ingredients for this board, I encourage you to forage your refrigerator and make use of those leftovers. Substitute any veggies with ones that are in season and use chickpeas or tofu for vegetarian options.

FOR THE BOARD:

20-inch (51-cm) food board

1 ½ cups (300 g) cooked brown rice

1 ½ cups (300 g) cooked farro

1 ½ cups (300 g) cooked quinoa

3 cups (420 g) cubed grilled chicken breast or rotisserie chicken

6 soft-boiled eggs

¾ cup (110 g) mozzarella cheese pearls

½ cup (60 g) crumbled goat cheese

⅓ cup (80 g) pickled onions (see Tip, page 74)

¼ cup (60 g) pesto

¼ cup (60 ml) toasted sesame dressing

¼ cup (60 ml) lemon vinaigrette

1 bunch asparagus, blanched

2 ½ cups (400 g) roasted potatoes

1 ¼ cups (225 g) roasted sweet potatoes

1 cup (110 g) shredded carrot

1 cup (150 g) cherry tomatoes, halved

1 cup (100 g) snap peas, cut into chunks

1 ½ cups (45 g) Tuscan kale, sautéed

1 cup (150 g) corn kernels

½ cup (15 g) parsley, for garnish

BOARD ASSEMBLY:

1. Place any hot pads or trivets on the board for the hot grain bowls.

2. Fill 8 bowls with the rice, farro, quinoa, cooked chicken, soft-boiled eggs, mozzarella, goat cheese, and pickled onion. Fill 3 very small bowls with the pesto and the dressings. Place the bowls on the board.

3. Fill in open areas with the cooked asparagus, roasted potatoes, roasted sweet potatoes, carrot, cherry tomatoes, snap peas, kale, and corn.

4. Tuck the fresh parsley around the board as garnish and add a sprig to the grain bowls.

YIELD: 6 servings

CHAPTER 7

Don't Forget Dessert!

Remember when people used to come over for dessert? I remember my parents hosting dessert nights. It was such a fun and easy way to bring people together. Because really, who doesn't love dessert? Nothing looks or tastes as inviting as a board of decadent desserts, so I say it's time to bring back dessert night!

The Pound Cake French Toast Board will make your house smell like heaven. So will the Berry Crumble Board! The Scoopin' Ice Cream Donut Sundae Board and the Chocolate Fondue Board are always big hits that bring out the kid in everybody. Speaking of kids, desserts boards are a wonderful way to encourage budding chefs because kids love making dessert boards!

CAKE BITES DESSERT BOARD

Host an old-fashioned dessert night and serve this board with hot drinks. This is an easy and delicious board for any holiday or special occasion. Just stop off at your local bakery for cake bites and you're nearly done! Create your own design by laying down the cake bites first, and then filling in with the fruit. Guests will love creating their own dessert masterpieces.

FOR THE BOARD:

26-inch (66-cm) food board

Best Whipped Cream (see Tip)

1 cup (240 ml) caramel dip

13 ounces (364 g) mini cinnamon rolls

13 ounces (364 g) cheesecake bites

13 ounces (364 g) pumpkin cake bites

13 ounces (364 g) chocolate cake bites

1 pound (454 g) pecan tarts

4 cups (600 g) red grapes

2 cups (300 g) green grapes

2 whole pears, for garnish

2 red pears, cored and sliced

2 green apples, cored and sliced

2 red apples, cored and sliced

3 to 4 ounces (84 to 112 g) dark chocolate pieces

BOARD ASSEMBLY:

1. Place a bowl in the center of the board with the whipped cream. Fill a second bowl with the caramel dip and place on the board.

2. Make your own design with the cinnamon rolls, cake bites, and tarts. Place the grapes in 5 or 6 clusters on the board. Lay down the whole pears for garnish. Fill in open areas with the pear and apple slices and the chocolate pieces.

YIELD: 16 to 24 servings

TIP: For the Best Whipped Cream: In a bowl with a hand mixer or in a stand mixer, whip 1 cup (240 ml) heavy cream until thickened, 3 or 4 minutes. Add ¼ cup (60 g) crème fraîche, ¼ cup (30 g) powdered sugar, ½ teaspoon vanilla extract, and a pinch of salt and whip again until combined and creamy.

POUND CAKE FRENCH TOAST BOARD

In case you couldn't tell, I strongly believe breakfast can, and should, be served for any meal of the day, including dessert. One night while craving breakfast for dessert, I dreamt up the idea of combining pound cake and French toast, and thus this recipe was born. Get out your favorite ice cream, whip up some cream, put out some berries, and indulge in this breakfast-inspired board.

FOR THE BOARD:

20-inch (51-cm) food board

Pound Cake French Toast (recipe follows)

1 recipe Best Whipped Cream (see Tip, page 153)

½ cup (120 g) Nutella

2 cups (300 g) fresh strawberries, sliced

2 cups (300 g) fresh blueberries

2 cups (300 g) fresh raspberries

FOR THE POUND CAKE FRENCH TOAST:

5 large egg yolks

1 large egg

1 cup (240 ml) heavy cream

¾ cup (180 ml) half-and-half

⅓ cup (65 g) granulated sugar

1 teaspoon vanilla extract

1 teaspoon cinnamon

¾ teaspoon kosher salt

Pinch of freshly grated nutmeg

¼ cup (60 g) unsalted butter, melted and divided

1 12 ounces (42 g) pound cake loaf, cut into 6 to 8 slices

¼ cup (50 g) brown sugar

¼ cup (30 g) powdered sugar

BOARD ASSEMBLY:

1. Place a hot pad in the center of the board to hold a 9 x 13-inch (23 x 33-cm) pan for the French toast.

2. Just before you are ready to serve, fill bowls with the whipped cream and Nutella. Set on one side of the board. Arrange the fruit around the outside of the board. Place the baked French toast on the hot pad.

POUND CAKE FRENCH TOAST:

1. In a large mixing bowl, combine the egg yolks, egg, heavy cream, half-and-half, granulated sugar, vanilla, cinnamon, salt, and nutmeg. Whisk until combined and set aside.

2. Pour 2 tablespoons (30 ml) of the melted butter into the bottom of a 9 x 13-inch (23 x 33-cm) pan. Pour in about one-third of the egg mixture, then add the pound cake slices in a single layer on top. Pour the remaining egg mixture on top and cover the pan with plastic wrap. Soak the cake for at least 4 hours before baking.

3. Preheat the oven to 350°F (180°C, or gas mark 4). Mix the brown sugar and remaining 2 tablespoons (30 ml) melted butter together and gently spread onto each piece of cake with the back of a spoon. Cover with foil and bake for 30 minutes. Uncover the pan and bake for an additional 10 to 12 minutes, then broil on low for 2 to 3 more minutes until the brown sugar is golden and crunchy.

4. Right before serving, sprinkle the French toast with the powdered sugar.

YIELD: 6 to 8 servings

CHOCOLATE FONDUE BOARD

Raise your hand if you also have a drawer in your kitchen solely dedicated to chocolate—I certainly do. Clearly, I'm a shameless fanatic for any form of chocolate—a simple bar, spreadable Nutella, or decadent flourless chocolate cake. Chocolate pairs well with literally anything (hello, bacon and potato chips), which is why I made this board. You can compile your favorite, dippable chocolate companions onto a dessert board that satiates everyone. If you're in a pinch for time, everything but the fondue can be store-bought.

FOR THE BOARD:

26-inch (66-cm) food board

2 cups (480 g) Nutella or hazelnut spread

2 cups (480 ml) heavy cream

2 tablespoons (20 g) dark chocolate chips

½ cup (120 g) peanut butter, divided

2 tablespoons (12 g) peanuts

24 French macarons

12 ounces (336 g) raspberries

8 ounces (224 g) small waffles

8 ounces (224 g) large marshmallows

8 ounces (224 g) brownie bites

2 pounds (908 g) strawberries

1 pound cake, cut into 1-inch (2.5-cm) pieces

12 ounces (336 g) blackberries

8 ounces (224 g) pretzel bites

8 ounces (224 g) pink and white shortbread cookies

15 ounces (420 g) cheesecake wedges, cut into small slices

BOARD ASSEMBLY:

1. To make the chocolate fondue, warm the Nutella in the microwave oven. Heat the heavy cream in a separate bowl at high power for 45 seconds, or until very hot. Slowly whisk the cream into the bowl of Nutella, until very smooth. Allow to sit and thicken up.

2. Divide the fondue between 2 medium bowls. Sprinkle one bowl with the chocolate chips. Mix ¼ cup (60 g) peanut butter into the other bowl, then swirl the remaining ¼ cup (60 g) on top and sprinkle with the peanuts. Place the 2 bowls on the board.

3. Around the inside edge of the board, make wedges in a circular pattern, starting with the macarons. Then add the raspberries, small waffles, marshmallows, brownie bites, strawberries, pound cake bites, blackberries, pretzel bites, cookies, and cheesecake slices.

YIELD: 12 or more servings

TIP: Make the fondue ahead and store in the fridge. Right before serving, heat on the stovetop over low heat or in the microwave at 50 percent power until warm.

SCOOPIN' ICE CREAM DONUT SUNDAE BOARD

For this board, I wanted to take the classic ice cream sundae to the next level by adding one of my favorite desserts: donuts. They're not often eaten with ice cream, but after you try this board, you'll be wondering why you haven't eaten a donut sundae sooner. To prepare ahead of time, scoop and freeze the ice cream and donuts together on a parchment-lined baking sheet—the donuts will take on a firmer texture, but still taste just as delicious.

FOR THE BOARD:

20-inch (51-cm) food board

1 recipe Best Whipped Cream (see Tip, page 153)

6 Oreos, crushed

½ cup (60 g) rainbow sprinkles

½ cup (120 g) hot fudge

3 sugar cones, crushed

4 peanut butter cups, roughly chopped

⅓ cup (45 g) roasted peanuts

8 powdered donuts

8 glazed donuts

2 bananas, peeled and quartered

2 cups (300 g) fresh cherries

2 cups (300 g) strawberries, halved

1 pint (480 g) pistachio ice cream

1 pint (480 g) vanilla ice cream

1 pint (480 g) chocolate peanut butter ice cream

1 pint (480 g) strawberry ice cream

BOARD ASSEMBLY:

1. Place a bowl that will hold the whipped cream in the center of the board.

2. Fill 6 bowls with the Oreos, sprinkles, hot fudge, crushed sugar cones, peanut butter cups, and peanuts. Place the whipped cream in the center of the board, and these 6 bowls circled around it.

3. Around the inside edge of the board, lay down the powdered donuts on one side and the glazed on the other.

4. Where the two types of donuts meet, lay down the bananas in between. Fill in the open areas with the cherries and strawberries.

5. When ready to serve, fill 4 bowls with crushed ice and place the ice cream containers and ice cream scoops in each one.

YIELD: 8 servings

MAKE-YOUR-OWN TRIFLE CUPS BOARD

A boozy trifle is welcome on my table at any time of the year. Trifles can be light, fluffy, and fruity, or rich, decadent, and chocolatey: this board has ingredients for any trifle variation. Make this for a celebration or holiday. Swap out different kinds of cakes, puddings, or toppings according to the season.

FOR THE BOARD:

26-inch (66-cm) food board

1 recipe Best Whipped Cream (see Tip, page 153)

2 cups (480 g) vanilla pudding

2 cups (480 g) chocolate pudding

¾ cup (180 g) lemon curd

1 can (29 ounces, or 812 g) canned peaches

1 can (15 ounces, or 420 g) dark sweet cherries

½ cup (70 g) pistachios, chopped

¾ cup (60 g) shredded coconut

14 ounces (392 g) pound cake, cut into 1-inch (2.5-cm) cubes

1½ pounds (680 g) brownie bites, cut into 1-inch (2.5-cm) cubes (half of a box mix)

12 ounces (336 g) fresh raspberries

1 pound (454 g) fresh blueberries

7 ounces (196 g) chocolate biscuits or cookies

6 ounces (168 g) vanilla wafers

¼ cup (60 ml) cream sherry (optional)

Fresh mint, for garnish

BOARD ASSEMBLY:

1. Place 3 large bowls on the board and fill with the whipped cream, vanilla pudding, and chocolate pudding. Fill 3 more bowls with the lemon curd, peaches, and cherries and place on the board. Place 2 smaller bowls with the chopped pistachios and coconut on the board.

2. Around the outside of the board, place the pound cake cubes. On the opposite side, place the brownie bites. Lay down the raspberries and blueberries across from each other. Fill the center of the board with the biscuits and wafers. Garnish with the fresh mint.

3. Instruct diners on how to make a trifle cup: On the bottom of an 8-ounce (224-g) clear cup, crumble wafers or biscuits. Alternate pudding, fruit, cake and brownie bites, and whipped cream. Top with pistachios and shredded coconut.

YIELD: 10 or more servings

TIP: If you want to add alcohol, use the sherry to soak canned or fresh fruit for a few hours, or overnight.

BERRY CRUMBLE BOARD

Here's an any-season dessert board that comes together in no time! People love to "make their own"—a little bit of this, a little bit of that. When this dessert comes out of the oven, serve it with soft vanilla ice cream. I keep premade crumble in my freezer at all times and you can too. Summer berries . . . we're coming for you!

FOR THE BOARD:

24 to 26-inch (60–66 cm) food board

Eight 1-cup (240-g) ramekins

Crumble (recipe follows)

1 cup (165 g) white chocolate chips

1 cup (165 g) chocolate chips

1 lemon, sliced

1 ¼ pounds (560 g) fresh strawberries, sliced

1 ¼ pounds (560 g) fresh blueberries

1 ¼ pounds (560 g) fresh raspberries

12 ounces (336 g) fresh blackberries

Edible flowers, for garnish (optional)

3 pints (500 g) vanilla ice cream

FOR THE CRUMBLE:

¾ cup (180 g) unsalted butter

1 cup (80 g) quick oats

1 cup (120 g) all-purpose flour

⅔ cup (130 g) brown sugar

½ cup (40 g) shredded coconut

1 teaspoon cardamom (optional)

1 teaspoon kosher salt

1 teaspoon vanilla extract

1 teaspoon orange or lemon zest (optional)

BOARD ASSEMBLY:

1. Place three medium-size bowls for the ice cream on the board. Place the ramekins around the board.

2. Place a bowl with the crumble on the board. Fill 3 small bowls with the chocolate chips and lemon slices and place them on the board. Add fresh berries to the open areas and arrange 1-cup (240-g) and ⅓ cup (80 g) measuring cups and edible flowers (if using) on top.

3. Preheat the oven to 375°F (190°C, or gas mark 5).

4. Instruct diners to fill their ramekin with 1 cup (150 g) fruit and squeeze lemon juice on top. Add ⅓ cup (80 g) crumble and chocolate chips if desired. Don't pat them down! Place the filled ramekins on a baking sheet (see Tip) and transfer to the oven. Bake for 30 to 35 minutes, until the crumble is golden and the fruit bubbles around the edges.

5. Just before serving the baked fruit crumble, add crushed ice to the medium-size bowls and place the ice cream pints in each one. Remove the crumble from the oven and let guests scoop their own ice cream!

CRUMBLE:

1. Mix all the ingredients for the crumble together and transfer to the bowl on the board.

YIELD: 8 servings

TIP: Make a note of which ramekin belongs to whom on a sheet of paper before baking, to ensure your guests get their personalized ramekin. Use frozen berries if you are in a pinch, but keep in mind, they will melt a little on the board.

FUNFETTI COOKIE DOUGH BOARD

When I was young, my friends and I had a way of getting caught with our hands in the cookie jar! Except the jar was a mixing bowl with unbaked cookies. I love cookie dough, sometimes more than the actual cookie. I think many kids feel similarly, which is why I created the Funfetti Cookie Dough Board. It's perfect for a child's birthday. But there is a twist, which you might not want to mention. The cookie dough is actually made with chickpeas and almond flour, making it gluten-free and higher in both fiber and protein than regular cookie dough—perfect for subduing a sugar rush. Additionally, I include two variations: a peanut butter base dough with chocolate and vanilla.

FOR THE BOARD:

20-inch (51-cm) food board

10 pieces Chickpea Cookie Dough, chocolate variation (recipe follows)

10 pieces Chickpea Cookie Dough, vanilla variation (recipe follows)
25 regular Oreo cookies
25 vanilla Oreo cookies

1 cup (240 g) hot fudge

½ cup (120 g) pitted Amarena cherries with stems and juice

10 ice cream sugar cones

6 ounces (168 g) fresh raspberries

15 strawberries, halved

FOR THE CHICKPEA COOKIE DOUGH:

1 cup (240 ml) almond or other nut milk, divided

1 tablespoon (15 g) unsalted butter

2 cans (15 ounces, or 420 g) unseasoned chickpeas, drained and rinsed

½ cup (60 g) plus 3 tablespoons (25 g) almond flour

⅓ cup (65 g) coconut sugar

¼ cup (60 g) honey

1 teaspoon vanilla extract

¾ cup (180 g) peanut butter or other nut or seed butter

1 ½ teaspoons kosher salt, plus more to taste

1 teaspoon baking soda

BOARD ASSEMBLY:

1. Place 2 plates on the board to hold the cookie dough. Fan the regular Oreo cookies around the vanilla cookie dough plate. Fan the vanilla Oreo cookies around the chocolate cookie dough plate.

2. Place bowls with the hot fudge and the cherries on the board. Lay the sugar cones on one side and fill in the open spaces with the raspberries and strawberries. Right before serving, place the chilled cookie dough on the plates.

CHICKPEA COOKIE DOUGH:

1. In a medium saucepan, combine ¾ cup (180 ml) of the nut milk, the butter, and the chickpeas, bring to a boil, then reduce to a simmer, cover with a lid, and cook over medium-low heat until the chickpeas start to fall apart, and the liquid evaporates, 10 to 12 minutes.

2. Transfer the chickpeas to a food processor along with the almond flour, coconut sugar, honey, vanilla, peanut butter, salt, baking soda, and remaining ¼ cup (60 ml) nut milk. Blend until very smooth and creamy, scraping the sides as needed, for 6 to 8 minutes. Season with salt to taste.

3. Remove the dough from the food processor, wrap it in plastic, and chill in the refrigerator for about an hour.

4. When the dough is at room temperature or cooler, stir in the sprinkles. Divide the dough in half.

⅓ cup (40 g) rainbow sprinkles (see Tip)

¼ cup (30 g) cocoa powder and ⅓ cup (55 g) dark chocolate chips (for chocolate variation)

⅓ cup (55 g) white chocolate chips (for vanilla variation)

5. For chocolate dough, mix in the cocoa and dark chocolate chips. For the vanilla dough, mix in the white chocolate chips.

6. Use a ¼-cup (60-g) cookie scoop to portion out the dough into 10 balls for each flavor. Place the balls on a parchment-lined plate, cover with plastic wrap, and place in the freezer for 30 minutes; this helps the balls keep their shape and prevent sticking.

YIELD: 10 or more servings

TIP: If you want a swirled look, add the sprinkles while the dough is still warm. You can also mix in other ingredients, such as shredded coconut, dried fruit, and seeds.

WONDERFUL WAFFLE DESSERT BOARD

In my opinion, waffles are appropriate to eat for any meal of the day, especially dessert. While waffles and ice cream make a delicious combo, waffles and Bananas Foster can be even better. Bananas are caramelized in a syrup of butter and brown sugar warmed by nutmeg and cinnamon. The best part of this flambé dessert? Wowing your guests with a light show by igniting the white rum before serving on the board.

FOR THE BOARD:

20-inch (51-cm) food board

Bananas Foster (recipe follows)

1 recipe Best Whipped Cream (see Tip, page 153)

12 petite Belgian waffles, warmed

½ cup (120 g) hot fudge

¼ cup (35 g) pistachios

¼ cup (20 g) shredded coconut

4 cups (600 g) strawberries

3 cups (450 g) blueberries

FOR THE BANANAS FOSTER:

½ cup (120 g) unsalted butter

1 cup (200 g) packed brown sugar

½ teaspoon cinnamon

Pinch of freshly grated nutmeg

1 teaspoon vanilla extract

½ teaspoon kosher salt, or to taste

6 bananas, peeled and quartered lengthwise

¼ cup (60 ml) white rum (optional)

2 tablespoons (30 ml) heavy cream

¼ cup (30 g) walnuts, toasted (see Tip)

BOARD ASSEMBLY:

1. Place a trivet on the board to hold the Bananas Foster. Fill another bowl with the whipped cream and place on the board. Arrange the waffles, 6 on each side, around the trivet.

2. Fill 3 small bowls with the hot fudge, pistachios, and coconut. Place in the center of the board. Fill in open spaces with the strawberries on one side and the blueberries on the other.

3. Right before serving, place the hot Bananas Foster on the trivet.

BANANAS FOSTER:

1. In a large skillet over medium-high heat, melt the butter and brown sugar until the sugar has dissolved. Add the cinnamon, nutmeg, vanilla, and salt and stir to combine.

2. Place the bananas in the pan, cut side down, and baste with the syrup. Cook over medium heat until the bananas are softened and caramelized, about 4 minutes. If you're adding the rum, pour it over the bananas and, very carefully, ignite the liquor. Cook until the flame dies, then remove from the heat.

3. Transfer to a serving dish, drizzle with the heavy cream, and sprinkle with the walnuts.

YIELD: 6 servings

TIP: How to toast walnuts: Place the walnuts on a paper towel and microwave on high for 45 seconds. Rearrange and heat again for another 30 to 45 seconds. You do not want them to burn. Continue until toasted.

ACKNOWLEDGMENTS

To my loyal readers. Your energy and enthusiasm for *The Big Board* is why this book exists today. Thank you for sharing the same passion for hosting and feeding your family as I do.

To my blogging sisters. The Big Board concept began with an epic charcuterie in 2017 during your visit to Oregon. Little did we know "The Big Board" phenomenon would inspire so many! Thank you for being a part of those "first bites": Lori, Gina, Heidi, Maria, Brenda, Cathy, Cheryl, Mary, Erin, Amanda, and Kristen!

To Abby. Thank you, beautiful daughter, for your passion and creativity, pairings and food-styling skills. Your spectacular photography is a work of art, and it will take you far.

To my kitchen BFF and dog whisperer, Kristy. Oh, the endless hours of laughter and creating and serving boards together! Thank you for standing beside me, helping me play with food, and tenderly telling Alder "No." #TeamKrindy

To Cyndi (a.k.a. Hyacinth, The Pioneer Woman's BFF). From the moment we met, we were kindred spirits. I can never thank you enough for your partnership on The Big Board. What I've learned from you has been irreplaceable.

To Barb. Who would have thought that fifteen years ago we'd meet through the internet, a book, and a box of lamb?

To Marie. My fellow author and happy hour friend, thank you *both* for the many edits.

To Lori, Cathy, and Cheryl. Thank you for daily texts, reminders that hard work pays off, and for many years of friendship and blogging advice.

To Cindy, Jenny, and Kristi. I'll never forget the laughter and our campfire brainstorm session.

To Laurel, for helping land the board themes. And thank you to my sisters, Diane and Linda, and my many recipe testers! A special thanks to Adrienne (Buzg).

To my editor, Lydia. Thank you from the very beginning for your love and support for this book. Thank you for keeping me on track, and for the rest of the incredible team at Quarto: Todd, Erik, John, and David.

To my agent, Cyle Young. What a joy to work with you. Thank you for vision and help.

To my fellow board-makers and cheese lovers: Meagan, Marissa, and Meg—you inspire me!

To my family—my husband, Paul, and Elliot, Garrett and Vicky, and Abby—you've always been my biggest fans and my favorite taste-testers (the good and the bad). We have the best memories of many meals together. Even though we're scattered across the world now, you are forever in my heart. Paul, I couldn't have pursued my blog and focused on the little golden nuggets of life without you. You're my best friend and always bring me back to what's important, and I love you for that. Your saying years ago, "Those who feed people, lead people," has helped me change the lives of many.

SOURCES THAT INSPIRE

BOARDS – CHOOSE YOUR SHAPE

The BIG BOARD by Reluctant Entertainer
www.houseofhyacinth.com

Round:
Big Board 26-inch
Big Board 20-inch
Big Board Lazy Susan 23-inch

Big Board Rectangular 12 x 36

SERVING WITH STYLE – UTENSILS, DISHES, AND MORE

Crate and Barrel
www.crateandbarrel.com

House of Hyacinth
www.houseofhyacinth.com

Lark Modern Home
www.larkmountainmodern.com

Le Creuset
www.lecreuset.com

Sur la Table
www.surlatable.com

Target
www.target.com

Williams Sonoma
www.williams-sonoma.com

World Market (Cost Plus)
www.worldmarket.com

Be Home
Found at www.houseofhyacinth.com

NOURISHMENT AND NOSHES

Amazon
www.amazon.com

Costco
www.costco.com

Delallo
www.delallo.com

Fred Meyer (Kroger)
www.fredmeyer.com

Market of Choice
www.marketofchoice.com

Newport Avenue Market

www.newportavenuemarket.com
Trader Joe's
www.traderjoes.com

Uwajimaya
www.uwajimaya.com

Walmart
www.walmart.com

Whole Foods
www.wholefoods.com

World Market (Cost Plus)
www.worldmarket.com

ABOUT THE AUTHOR

SANDY COUGHLIN writes about food, travel, and hospitality on her popular blog, Reluctant Entertainer. Her mission is to help readers feast on life by providing easy and tasty recipes, time-saving tips, and inspiration to help reluctant entertainers open their hearts and homes to others through great food and great conversations. Coughlin is the author of *The Reluctant Entertainer*. She has been featured by *Woman's Day*, *Rachael Ray*, *Better Homes and Gardens*, *Taste of Home*, and more. She enjoys hosting parties that create life-long connections and memories. She is a mother to three grown children and lives in Bend, Oregon, with her husband, Paul. You can find her on social media @ReluctantEntertainer.

PHOTOGRAPHER

ABBY COUGHLIN is a photographer based in the Pacific Northwest. After spending nearly ten years of practicing photography as a hobby, she decided to pursue it professionally after graduating from college with a degree in music. In addition to photography, she is also a budding food stylist and recipe developer. To her, there are few things more joy inducing than preparing a meal and sharing it with loved ones. She plans on continuing her love affair with food and photography for many years to come.

INDEX